PySide GUI Application Development

Second Edition

Develop more dynamic and robust GUI applications using PySide, an open source cross-platform UI framework

Gopinath Jaganmohan

Venkateshwaran Loganathan

PUBLISHING

BIRMINGHAM - MUMBAI

PySide GUI Application Development
Second Edition

First published: October 2013

Second Edition: January 2016

Production reference: 1200116

Published by Packt Publishing Ltd.
Livery Place
35 Livery Street
Birmingham B3 2PB, UK.

ISBN 978-1-78528-245-4

www.packtpub.com

Credits

Authors
Gopinath Jaganmohan
Venkateshwaran Loganathan

Reviewer
Sivan Greenberg

Commissioning Editor
Dipika Gaonkar

Acquisition Editors
Greg Wild
Meeta Rajani

Content Development Editor
Mamata Walkar

Technical Editor
Siddhesh Patil

Copy Editor
Priyanka Ravi

Project Coordinator
Shipra Chauhan

Proofreader
Safis Editing

Indexer
Monica Ajmera Mehta

Graphics
Disha Haria

Production Coordinator
Conidon Miranda

Cover Work
Conidon Miranda

About the Authors

Gopinath Jaganmohan is an Internet of Things evangelist and open source distributed-computing architect. He has 14 years of experience in various industries and has architected and lead implementation in Internet of Things platforms and solutions for enterprise in Telematics, Healthcare, and Wearables. He has worked on various technologies starting from C, Python, Lua, to Node.js, and implemented Big Data technologies like Hbase, Couchbase and ZooKeeper for various clients. He is passionate about device programming and device integration. He is lately working on deep learning technologies like Keras, scikit, Torch7 and Pandas in machine learning for device data.

Venkateshwaran Loganathan is an eminent software developer who has been involved in the design, development, and testing of software products for more than five years now. He was introduced to computer programming at an early age of 11 with FoxPro, and he then started to learn and master various computer languages, such as C, C++, Perl, Python, Node.js, and Unix shell scripting. Fascinated by open source development, he has involved himself in contributing to various open source technologies.

He is now working for Cognizant Technology Solutions as a technology specialist where he has involved himself in research and development for the Internet of Things domain. He is now actively involved in using RFID devices, Drones, and Google Glass to evolve Future of Technology concepts. Before joining with Cognizant, he worked with few of the IT majors, such as Infosys, Virtusa, and NuVeda. Starting his career as a network developer, he gained expertise in various domains, such as Networking, E-Learning, and HealthCare. He has won various awards and accolades to his merit in the companies he has worked for.

Venkateshwaran holds a bachelor's degree in Computer Science and Engineering from Anna University and an M.S in software systems from BITS, Pilani. Apart from programming, he is actively involved in handling various technical and soft skills classes for budding engineers and college students. His hobbies include singing and trekking. He likes to get involved with social servicing and move with people a lot. You can write to him at anandvenkat4@gmail.com.

I am indebted to many. First of all, I would like to thank my mother, Anbuselvi, and grandmother, Saraswathi, for their endless effort and perseverance in bringing me up to this level. I am thankful to the entire team at Packt for accepting my proposal in bringing out a book of this kind. I would like to especially mention Meeta, Neil, and Amigya for their valuable guidance throughout the writing of the manuscript.

I am very grateful to my technical reviewers, Oscar Campos, and Jibo He, for reviewing the manuscript and providing me with constructive feedback that helped me shape the content. I would also like to extend my sincere gratitude to my professors, Senthil Kumar, and Radhika, for guiding me and encouraging me in all my spheres of life. I would not be very kind if I missed thanking my sister, Kamala, and my aunt, Kalavathi, for all the hope and love they have towards me.

I would also like to thank all my friends and brothers as their list is too big to mention here. They all have been my well-wishers and helped me in my tough times. I have missed many people here, but my thanks are always due to them who directly or indirectly influenced my life.

Above all, thanks to The Almighty for the showers of blessings on me.

About the Reviewer

Sivan Greenberg has over 15 years of multidisciplinary information technology expertise and a sharp eye for quality. He became an open source contributor for the Debian project back in 2002, joining Ubuntu two years later. Sivan's contribution can be found, literally, all over the world of open source.

Sivan is a true jack of all trades with massive engineering and leadership experience. He uses Python for all of his development needs ever since it was pitched to him by The SABDFL and the Ubuntu community. Currently, he runs Vitakka.co, a rapid development consultancy firm together with a team of veterans of long open source fame. They enable start-ups to realize and implement their MVPs so that they can bootstrap quickly and easily by acquiring customers and getting noticed by VCs. The team's mastery of everything cloud, software, engineering, operations, and product management make this an extremely high quality game-changing process.

I would like to thank my Mom, Helena, and my family — Moshik, Shir, and Eric. You're the fuel that makes me tick. Mom, you planted and nurtured the seeds of knowledge in me.

www.PacktPub.com

Support files, eBooks, discount offers, and more

For support files and downloads related to your book, please visit www.PacktPub.com.

Did you know that Packt offers eBook versions of every book published, with PDF and ePub files available? You can upgrade to the eBook version at www.PacktPub.com and as a print book customer, you are entitled to a discount on the eBook copy. Get in touch with us at service@packtpub.com for more details.

At www.PacktPub.com, you can also read a collection of free technical articles, sign up for a range of free newsletters and receive exclusive discounts and offers on Packt books and eBooks.

https://www2.packtpub.com/books/subscription/packtlib

Do you need instant solutions to your IT questions? PacktLib is Packt's online digital book library. Here, you can search, access, and read Packt's entire library of books.

Why subscribe?

- Fully searchable across every book published by Packt
- Copy and paste, print, and bookmark content
- On demand and accessible via a web browser

Free access for Packt account holders

If you have an account with Packt at www.PacktPub.com, you can use this to access PacktLib today and view 9 entirely free books. Simply use your login credentials for immediate access.

Table of Contents

Preface   v

Chapter 1: Getting Started with PySide   1

Introducing PySide   2
Hello, GUI   2
Setting up PySide   4
Installing PySide using Windows   4
Installing PySide using Mac OS X   4
Installing PySide using Linux   5
Building PySide on Windows   6
Building PySide on Linux   7
   Prerequisites   7
Building PySide   7
   Mac OS X   8
Importing PySide objects   8
First PySide application   9
Exception handling as a practice   12
Summary   14

Chapter 2: Entering through Windows   15

Creating a simple window   15
Creating the application icon   19
Showing a tooltip   24
Adding a button   26
Centering the window on the screen   28
About box   29
Tracking time using timers   30
Windows style   34
Summary   35

Chapter 3: Main Windows and Layout Management   **37**

Creating the main window   **38**

Status bar   **39**

Menu bar   **43**

    The central widget   44

    Adding a menu bar   45

    Adding menus   46

Toolbar   **50**

Layout management   **50**

    Absolute positioning   51

    Layout containers   51

    QBoxLayout   52

      QHBoxLayout   53

      QVBoxLayout   54

    QGridLayout   55

    QFormLayout   56

    QStackedLayout   56

SDI and MDI   **57**

A simple text editor   **57**

Summary   **63**

Chapter 4: Events and Signals   **65**

Event management   **65**

    Event loop   66

    Event processing   67

      Reimplementing event handlers   67

      Installing event filters   71

      Reimplementing the notify() function   73

Signals and slots   **73**

Drag and drop technique   **78**

Drawing shapes   **80**

Graphics and effects   **83**

Summary   **86**

Chapter 5: Dialogs and Widgets   **87**

Built-in dialogs   **88**

    QFileDialog   88

    QInputDialog   91

    QColorDialog   93

    QPrintDialog   94

Custom dialogs   **95**

Widgets at a glance	**97**
Custom widget	**100**
Implementation of MDI	**102**
Summary	**104**
Chapter 6: Database Handling	**105**
Connecting to the database	**105**
Executing SQL queries	**107**
Executing a query	108
Inserting, updating and deleting records	108
Navigating records	110
Database transactions	111
Table and form views	**112**
QSqlQueryModel	112
QSqlTableModel	112
QSqlRelationalTableModel	113
Table view	**114**
Form view	**116**
Viewing relations in table views	**119**
Summary	**120**
Index	**121**

Preface

The aim of this book is to introduce you to developing GUI applications in an easy way. Python is easy to learn and use, and its programs are relatively short compared to those written in any other programming languages, such as C++, and Java. It is supported by a large set of dynamic libraries and bindings that make it efficient to develop very complex applications in an efficient manner. This book will introduce you to user interface programming and its components. You will be able to develop real-time applications in a shorter time after reading this book. The second edition.

What this book covers

Chapter 1, Getting Started with PySide, introduces you to GUI programming in general. This chapter takes you through the introduction of PySide and its installation in various major operating systems, followed by a short introduction to exception handling in programming. By the end of this chapter, users will know how to install and use PySide to create GUI applications in Python.

Chapter 2, Entering through Windows, introduces you to all the GUI programming that revolves around Windows. This chapter explains the basic methods of creating windows and adding some functions to them. By the end of this chapter, users will be familiar with how to create windows and modify them accordingly.

Chapter 3, Main Windows and Layout Management, elaborates further on the previous chapter by explaining how to create menus and tool bars for a windowed application. This also explains layout management policies. A simple text editor is given as an example at the end of the chapter. By the end of this chapter, readers have an experience of creating a real-time application in PySide.

Chapter 4, Events and Signals, this chapter goes on to explain the signals, various text and graphic effects, drag and drop, and a few geometrical diagram shapes. By the end of this chapter, readers will learn about managing events and various other text and graphical effects.

Chapter 5, *Dialogs and Widgets*, details the built-in dialog boxes for applications, introduces how to create customized dialogs, and then takes a look at the various widgets that are available in PySide. By the end of this chapter, you will learn about creating your own customized widgets and dialogs.

Chapter 6, *Database Handling*, explains how connecting to a database is evident for almost all applications. This chapter is dedicated to explaining how to connect to a database and execute queries on it. It also deals with the presentation of data in table and form views. By the end of this chapter, you will know more about interacting with databases and viewing data from them.

What you need for this book

To execute the examples that are provided in this book, you will require a standard installation of Python v2.6 or later, including Python v3.4, and PySide v1.0.7 or later. A good text editor application, such as Sublime Text, will also help in writing Python programs in an IDE environment.

Who this book is for

Are you a GUI developer or fascinated by GUI programming? Bored with writing several lines of code to create a simple button in GUI? Then this book is for you. This book is written for Python programmers to try their hands at GUI programming. Even if you are new to Python but have some programming experience with any of the object-oriented languages, you will be able to easily pick it up as Python is easy to learn.

Conventions

In this book, you will find a number of text styles that distinguish between different kinds of information. Here are some examples of these styles and an explanation of their meaning.

Code words in text are shown as follows: "The `import pyside` command should not return any errors".

A block of code is set as follows:

```
    # Import required modules
import sys, time
from PySide.QtGui import *
from PySide.QtCore import *
```

Any command-line input or output is written as follows:

```
brew install pyside
port-install pyXX-pyside
```

New terms and **important words** are shown in bold. Words that you see on the screen, in menus or dialog boxes for example, appear in the text like this: "On clicking **Next** in the subsequent windows, and finally clicking **Finish**".

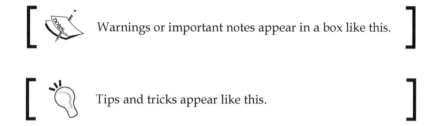

> Warnings or important notes appear in a box like this.

> Tips and tricks appear like this.

Reader feedback

Feedback from our readers is always welcome. Let us know what you think about this book—what you liked or disliked. Reader feedback is important for us as it helps us develop titles that you will really get the most out of.

To send us general feedback, simply e-mail feedback@packtpub.com, and mention the book's title in the subject of your message.

If there is a topic that you have expertise in and you are interested in either writing or contributing to a book, see our author guide at www.packtpub.com/authors.

Customer support

Now that you are the proud owner of a Packt book, we have a number of things to help you to get the most from your purchase.

Downloading the example code

You can download the example code files from your account at http://www.packtpub.com for all the Packt Publishing books you have purchased. If you purchased this book elsewhere, you can visit http://www.packtpub.com/support and register to have the files e-mailed directly to you.

Errata

Although we have taken every care to ensure the accuracy of our content, mistakes do happen. If you find a mistake in one of our books—maybe a mistake in the text or the code—we would be grateful if you could report this to us. By doing so, you can save other readers from frustration and help us improve subsequent versions of this book. If you find any errata, please report them by visiting http://www.packtpub.com/submit-errata, selecting your book, clicking on the **Errata Submission Form** link, and entering the details of your errata. Once your errata are verified, your submission will be accepted and the errata will be uploaded to our website or added to any list of existing errata under the Errata section of that title.

To view the previously submitted errata, go to https://www.packtpub.com/books/content/support and enter the name of the book in the search field. The required information will appear under the **Errata** section.

Piracy

Piracy of copyrighted material on the Internet is an ongoing problem across all media. At Packt, we take the protection of our copyright and licenses very seriously. If you come across any illegal copies of our works in any form on the Internet, please provide us with the location address or website name immediately so that we can pursue a remedy.

Please contact us at copyright@packtpub.com with a link to the suspected pirated material.

We appreciate your help in protecting our authors and our ability to bring you valuable content.

Questions

If you have a problem with any aspect of this book, you can contact us at questions@packtpub.com, and we will do our best to address the problem.

1
Getting Started with PySide

Python is a general-purpose, interpreted, object-oriented, and high-level programming language with dynamic semantics. It has efficient high-level data structures and a simple but effective approach to object-oriented programming. It is one of the most preferred programming languages by software developers due to its interpreted nature and its elegant syntax.

The success of Python lies in its simple and easy-to-learn syntax and the support of a wide variety of modules and packages that encourage program modularity and code reuse. Being an interpreted language, there is no compilation step, which makes the edit-test-debug cycle incredibly fast, paving the way to **Rapid Application Development**, the need of the hour. The support of object-oriented features and high-level data structures, such as generators and list comprehensions, makes Python a superior language for coding small scripting programs to more advanced game programming.

This book assumes that you have been acquainted with Python and want to test its capability in creating GUI applications. However, Python is easy to learn in just a week. If you already know programming, then learning Python will be like walking in the park for you. There are many resources available online and offline covering a wide range of topics. Being an open source language, Python is also supported by many programmers around the globe in the IRC system under the tag *#python*.

Python is named after the BBC show *Monty Python's Flying Circus* and has nothing to do with reptiles. Thus, making references to Monty Python skits in documentation is practiced and encouraged.

The Python newsgroup, `comp.lang.python`, and mailing list python-list at `https://mail.python.org/mailman/listinfo/python-list` will help you learn and explore Python.

Introducing PySide

Many of the modern programming languages are backed up by a set of libraries (commonly referred to as toolkits) to create GUI applications, such as Qt, Tcl/Tk, and so on. PySide is a Python binding of the cross-platform GUI toolkit Qt, and it runs on all platforms that are supported by Qt, including Windows, Mac OS X, and Linux. It is one of the alternatives to toolkits such as Tkinter for GUI programming in Python.

PySide combines the advantages of Qt and Python. A PySide programmer has all the power of Qt, but it is able to exploit it with the simplicity of Python. PySide is licensed under the LGPL version 2.1 license, allowing both Free/Open Source software and proprietary software development. PySide is evolving continuously, like any other open source product, and you are free to contribute to its development. Some of the applications, such as matplotlib, PhotoGrabber, QBitTorrent, Lucas Chess, Fminer and so on, certify the wide spread usage of PySide in the software industry.

 The IRC channel for PySide is #pyside at Freenode.

PySide has also become an enabler of mobile development. Qt Mobility is a project that is creating a new suite of Qt APIs for mobile device functionality. The project **Pyside Mobility** is a set of bindings that allows Python to access the Qt Mobility API. The Qt Mobility API enables the developer to access the bread and butter of services provided by the underlying operating system that are essential for any mobile application. Learning PySide, you learn this for free. Without further ado, let's get hacking!

Hello, GUI

In computing terms, **GUI** (pronounced as gooey, or **Graphical User Interface**) is used to denote a set of interfaces with computing systems that involves user-friendly images rather than boring text commands. GUI comes to the rescue of the numerous command-line interfaces that have always been coupled with a steep learning curve because learning and mastering commands requires a lot of effort due to their nonintuitive nature. Moreover, GUI layers make it easy for the end users to fulfill their needs without knowing much about the underlying implementation, which is unnecessary for them.

Every other application in the modern world is designed with interactive graphics to attract the end users. Simplicity and usability are the two main ingredients for a successful GUI system. The demanding feature of a GUI is to allow the user to concentrate on the task at hand. To achieve this, it must serve the interaction between the human and the computer, and make it no less than seamless and flowing. Therefore, learning to create GUIs will not only make you a successful developer, but it will also help in getting some revenue for yourself.

At a very basic level, a GUI is seen as a window (visibly noticeable or not) consisting of the following parts: controls, menu, layout, and interaction. A GUI is represented as a window on the screen and contains a number of different controls, as follows:

- **Controls**: These can, for example, be labels, buttons or text boxes.
- **Menu**: This is usually situated under the top frame of the GUI window and presents to the users some choices to control the application. The top frame can also have buttons to hide, resize, or destroy the windows, which are, again, controls.
- **Layout**: This is the way that the controls are positioned, which is very important in good GUI design.
- **Interaction**: This happens in the way of I/O devices, such as a mouse and keyboard.

Development of a GUI application revolves around defining and controlling these components, and designing the area of interaction is the most challenging part of all. The correct exploitation of events, listeners, and handlers will help in developing better GUI applications. Many frameworks have been developed to support GUI development, such as the Model-View-Controller framework that is used in many web-based applications. Using some of these frameworks can make the GUI programming easier and will come in handy for future implementations. A good user-interface design relates to the user, not to the system architecture.

 Usually, GUIs are characterized by 2W's, namely **WIMP** and **WYSIWYG**. They are acronyms for Windows, Icons, Menus, Pointing devices (mouse, joystick, and so on) and **What You See Is What You Get**.

Setting up PySide

This is your first step in this series of learning. PySide is compatible with Python 2.6 or later and Qt 4.6 or better. So, before getting to install PySide, we must make sure that minimum version compatibility is achieved. This section will teach you two ways of installing PySide. One, being the most common and easiest way, is using simple point and click installers and package managers. This will install the most stable version of PySide on your system, which you can comfortably use without worrying too much about the stability. However, if you are an advanced programmer, you may prefer to build PySide from scratch from the latest builds that are available when you are reading this book. Both these methods are explained here for Windows, Mac OS X, and Linux systems, and you are free to choose your own setup style.

Installing PySide using Windows

Installation of PySide on Windows is pretty much easy with the help of an installer. Perform the following steps for setup:

1. Get the latest stable package matching your Operating System architecture and the Python version installed from the releases page at `http://qt-project.org/wiki/PySide_Binaries_Windows`

2. Run the downloaded installer executable, which will automatically detect the Python installation from your system

3. You are given an option to install PySide on the default path or at the path of your choice

4. On clicking **Next** in the subsequent windows, and finally clicking **Finish**, PySide is installed successfully on your system

Installing PySide using Mac OS X

The binaries for MAC OS X installers of PySide are available at:

`http://qt-project.org/wiki/PySide_Binaries_MacOSX`

Download the latest version that is compatible with your system and perform a similar installation as explained in the previous section.

You can also choose to install PySide from the command line with the help of **Homebrew** or using **MacPorts**. The commands, respectively, are as follows:

```
brew install pyside
port-install pyXX-pyside
```

Replace xx with your Python version.

Installing PySide using Linux

Installing PySide on a Debian-based system is much easier with the synaptic package manager. Issuing the following command will fetch and install the latest stable version available in the aptitude distribution:

```
sudo apt-get install python-pyside
```

On an RPM-based system, you can use the RPM-based distribution, yum, as follows:

```
yum install python-pyside pyside-tools
```

If you want to make sure that PySide is installed properly on your system, issue the following commands in the Python shell environment, as shown in *Figure 1*. The `import pyside` command should not return any errors.

`PySide.__version__` should output something similar to `1.1.2`:

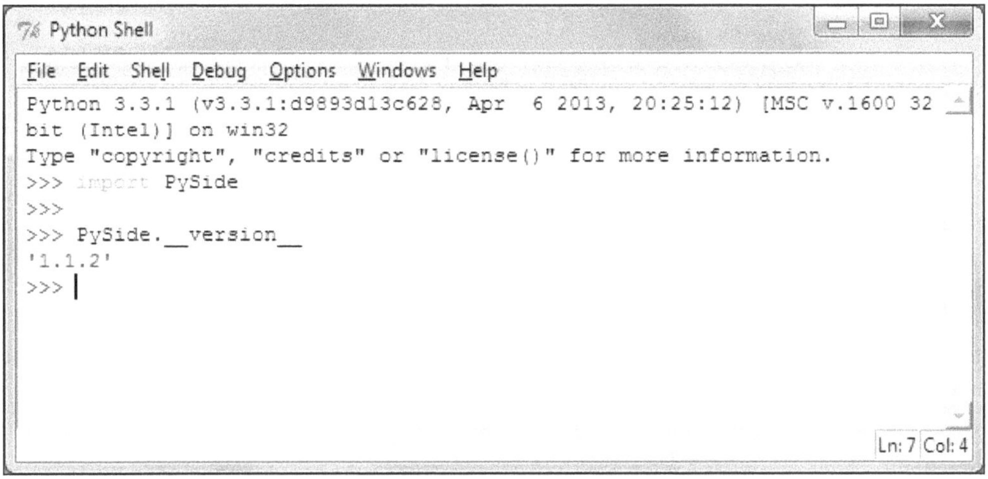

Figure 1

Let's move on to see how we can build PySide from scratch.

Building PySide on Windows

Before starting to build PySide on Windows, ensure that the following prerequisites are installed:

- Visual Studio Express 2008 (Python 2.6, 2.7, or 3.2) / Visual Studio Express 2010 (Python 3.3) [http://www.microsoft.com/visualstudio/eng/products/visual-studio-express-products]
- Qt 4.8 libraries for Windows [http://releases.qt-project.org/qt4/source/qt-win-opensource-4.8.4-vs2008.exe]
- CMake [http://www.cmake.org/cmake/resources/software.html]
- Git [http://git-scm.com/download/win]
- Python 2.6, 2.7, 3.2, or 3.3 [http://www.python.org/download/]
- OpenSSL [http://slproweb.com/products/Win32OpenSSL.html] (Optional)

Make sure that the Git and cmake executables are set in your system path. Now, perform the following steps to start building PySide:

1. Git Clone the PySide repository from GitHub, as follows:

   ```
   c:/> git clone https://github.com/PySide/pyside-setup.git pyside-setup
   ```

2. Change your working directory to `pyside-setup`, as follows:

   ```
   c:/> cd pyside-setup
   ```

3. Build the installer:

   ```
   c:\> c:\Python27\python.exe setup.py bdist_wininst --msvc-version=9.0 --make=c:\Qt\4.8.4\bin\qmake.exe --openssl=c:\OpenSSL32bit\bin
   ```

4. Upon successful installation, the binaries can be found in the `dist` sub-folder:

   ```
   c:\pyside-setup\dist
   ```

On completion of these steps, the PySide should have been successfully built on your system.

Building PySide on Linux

The following are the prerequisites to build PySide in Linux:

Prerequisites

- CMake version 2.6.0 or higher [http://www.cmake.org/cmake/resources/software.html]

- Qt libraries and development headers version 4.6 or higher [http://origin.releases.qt-project.org/qt4/source/qt-everywhere-opensource-src-4.8.4.tar.gz]

- libxml2 and development headers version 2.6.32 or higher [http://www.xmlsoft.org/downloads.html]

- libxslt and development headers version 1.1.19 or higher [http://xmlsoft.org/XSLT/downloads.html]

- Python libraries and development headers version 2.5 or higher [http://www.python.org/download/]

Building PySide

PySide is a collection of four interdependent packages, namely API Extractor, Generator Runner, Shiboken Generator, and Pyside Qt bindings. In order to build PySide, you have to download and install these packages in that order:

- **API Extractor**: This is a set of libraries that is used by the binding generator to parse the header and type system files to create an internal representation of the API [https://distfiles.macports.org/apiextractor/].

- **Generator Runner**: This is the program that controls the bindings generation process according to the rules given by the user through headers, type system files, and generator frontends. It is dependent on the API Extractor [https://distfiles.macports.org/generatorrunner/].

- **Shiboken Generator**: This is the plugin that creates the PySide bindings source files from Qt headers and auxiliary files (type systems, global.h, and glue files). It is dependent on Generator Runner and API Extractor [https://distfiles.macports.org/py-shiboken/].

- **PySide Qt Bindings**: This is a set of type system definitions and glue codes that allows generation of Python Qt binding modules using the PySide tool chain. It is dependent on Shiboken and Generator Runner [https://distfiles.macports.org/py-pyside/].

Always, make sure that you have downloaded and built these packages in this order because each of these packages is interdependent. The build steps for each of these are:

1. Unzip the downloaded packages and change into the package directory:

    ```
    tar -xvf <package_name>

    cd <package_directory>
    ```

2. Create a build directory under the package directory and enter that directory:

    ```
    mkdir build && cd build
    ```

3. Make the build using cmake:

    ```
    cmake .. && make
    ```

4. On a successful make, build and install the package:

    ```
    sudo make install
    ```

    Please note that you require sudo permissions to install the packages.

5. To update the runtime linker cache, issue the following command:

    ```
    sudo ldconfig
    ```

Once you complete these steps in this order for each of these packages, PySide should be successfully built on your system.

Mac OS X

Building PySide on a Mac system follows the same procedure as the Linux system except that Mac needs Xcode-Developer Tools to be installed as a prerequisite.

> If you are installing the libraries in a nondefault system directory (other than /usr/local), you may have to update the DYLD_LIBRARY_PATH by typing the following command:
> ```
> export DYLD_LIBRARY_PATH=~/my_dir/install/lib
> ```

Importing PySide objects

Congratulations on setting up Pyside successfully on your system. Now, it's time to do some real work using PySide. We have set up PySide and now we want to use it in our application. To do this, you have to import the PySide modules in your program to access the PySide data and functions. Here, let's learn some basics of importing modules in your Python program.

There are basically two ways that are widely followed when importing modules in Python. The first is to use a direct `import <module>` statement. This statement will import the module and creates a reference to the *module* in the current namespace. If you have to refer to entities (functions and data) that are defined in module, you can use `module.function`. The second is to use `from module import*`. This statement will import all of the entities that the module provides and set up references in the current namespace to all the public objects defined by that module. In this case, referencing an object within the module will boil down to simply stating its literal name in code.

Therefore, in order to use PySide functions and data in your program, you have to import it by saying either `import PySide` or `from PySide import*`. In the former case, if you have to refer to some function from PySide you have to prefix it with PySide, such as `PySide.<function_name>`. In the latter, you can simply call the function by `<function_name>`. Also, please note that in the latter statement, `*` can be replaced by specific functions or objects. The use of `*` denotes that we are trying to import all the available functions from that module. Throughout this book, I would prefer to use the latter format as I do not have to prefix the module name every time when I have to refer to something inside that module.

First PySide application

It's time to roll up our sleeves and get our hands dirty with some real coding now. We are going to learn how to create our first and the traditional `Hello World` application. Have a look at the code first, and we will dissect the program line by line for a complete explanation of what it does. The code may look a little strange to you at first but you will gain understanding as we move through:

```python
# Import the necessary modules required
import sys
from PySide.QtCore import *
from PySide.QtGui import *

# Main Function
if __name__ == '__main__':

    # Create the main application
    myApp = QApplication(sys.argv)

    # Create a Label and set its properties
    appLabel = QLabel()
    appLabel.setText("Hello, World!!!\n Look at my first app using PySide")
```

```
appLabel.setAlignment(Qt.AlignCenter)
appLabel.setWindowTitle("My First Application")
appLabel.setGeometry(300, 300, 250, 175)

# Show the Label
appLabel.show()

# Execute the Application and Exit
myApp.exec_()
sys.exit()
```

On interpretation, you will get an output window, as shown in the figure:

Now, let's get into the working of the code. We start with importing the necessary objects into the program.

Lines 1, 2 and 3 imports the necessary modules that are required for the program. Python is supported with a library of standard modules that are built into the interpreter and provide access to operations that are not a part of the core language. One such standard module is `sys`, which provides access to some variables and functions that are used closely by the interpreter. In the preceding program, we need the `sys` module to pass command-line arguments `sys.argv` as a parameter to the `QApplication` class. It contains the list of command-line arguments that are passed to a Python script. Any basic GUI application that uses PySide should have two classes imported for basic functionality. They are `QtCore` and `QtGui`. The `QtCore` module contains functions that handle signals and slots and overall control of the application, whereas `QtGui` contains methods to create and modify various GUI window components and widgets.

In the main program, we are creating an instance of the QApplication class. QApplication creates the main event loop, where all events from the window system and other sources are processed and dispatched. This class is responsible for an application's initialization, finalization, and session management. It also handles the events and sets the application's look and feel. It parses the command-line arguments (sys.argv) and sets its internal state, accordingly. There should be only one QApplication object in the whole application even though the application creates one or many windows at any point in time.

> The QApplication object must be created before the creation of any other objects as this handles system-wide and application-wide settings for your application. It is also advised to create it before any modification of command-line arguments is received.

Once the main application instance is created, we move on by creating a QLabel instance that will display the required message on the screen. This class is used to display a text or an image. The appearance of the text or image can be controlled in many ways by the functions provided by this class. The next two lines that follow the instantiation of this class set the text to be displayed and align it in a way that is centered on the application window.

As Python is an object-oriented programming language, we take the advantage of many object-oriented features, such as polymorphism, inheritance, object initialization, and so on. The complete Qt modules are designed in an object-oriented paradigm that supports these features. QLabel is a base class that is inherited from the QFrame super class whose parent class is QWidget (the details will be covered in forthcoming chapters). So, the functions that are available in QWidget and QFrame are inherited to QLabel. The two functions, setWindowTitle and setGeometry, are functions of QWidget, which are inherited by the QLabel class. These are used to set the title of the window and position it on the screen.

Now that all the instantiation and setup is done, we are calling the show function of the QLabel object to present the label on the screen. At this point only, the label becomes visible to the user and they are able to view it on the screen. Finally, we call the exec_() function of the QApplication object, which will enter the Qt main loop and start executing the Qt code. In reality, this is where the label will be shown to the user but the details can be safely ignored as of now. Finally, we exit the program by calling sys.exit().

Exception handling as a practice

It is not always possible to foresee all the errors in your programs and deal with them. Python comes with an excellent feature called **exception handling** to deal with all runtime errors. The aim of the book is not to explain this feature in detail but to give you some basic ideas so that you can implement it in the code that you write.

In general, the exceptions that are captured while executing a program are handled by saving the current state of the execution in a predefined place and switching the execution to a specific subroutine known as **exception handler**. Once they are handled successfully, the program takes the normal execution flow using the saved information. Sometimes, the normal flow may be hindered due to some exceptions that could not be resolved transparently. In any case, exception handling provides a mechanism for smooth flow of the program altogether.

In Python, the exception handling is carried out in a set of try and except statements. The try statements consist of a set of suspicious code that we think may cause an exception. On hitting an exception, the statement control is transferred to the except block where we can have a set of statements that handles the exception and resolves it for a normal execution of a program. The syntax for the same is as follows:

```
try : suite
except exception <, target> : suite
except : suite
```

Here, suite is an indented block of statements. We can also have a set of `try`, `except` block in a try suite. The former except statement provides a specific exception class that can be matched with the exception that is raised. The latter except statement is a general clause that is used to handle a catch-all version. It is always advisable to write our code in the exception encapsulation.

In the previous example, consider that we have missed instantiating the `appLabel` object. This might cause an exception confronting to a class of exception called `NameError`. If we did not encapsulate our code within the try block, this raises a runtime error. However, if we had put our code in a try block, an exception can be raised and handled separately, which will not cause any hindrance to the normal execution of the program. The following set of code explains this with the possible output:

```
# Import the necessary modules required
import sys
from PySide.QtCore import *
from PySide.QtGui import *
```

```
# Main Function
if __name__ == '__main__':

    # Create the main application
    myApp = QApplication(sys.argv)

    # Create a Label and set its properties
    try:
        #appLabel = QLabel()
        appLabel.setText("Hello, World!!!\n Look at my first app using
PySide")
        appLabel.setAlignment(Qt.AlignCenter)
        appLabel.setWindowTitle("My First Application")
        appLabel.setGeometry(300, 300, 250, 175)

        # Show the Label
        appLabel.show()

        # Execute the Application and Exit
        myApp.exec_()
        sys.exit()
    except NameError:
        print("Name Error:", sys.exc_info()[1])
        pass
```

In the preceding program, if we did not handle the exceptions, the output would be as shown in the figure:

Conversely, if we execute the preceding code, we will not run into any of the errors shown in the preceding figure. Instead, we will have captured the exception and given some information about it to the user, as follows:

```
74 Python Shell                                                    ⊡ X

File  Edit  Shell  Debug  Options  Windows  Help
Python 3.3.1 (v3.3.1:d9893d13c628, Apr  6 2013, 20:25:12) [MSC v.1600 32 bit (In
tel)] on win32
Type "copyright", "credits" or "license()" for more information.
>>> ================================ RESTART ================================
>>>
Name Error: name 'appLabel' is not defined
>>> |



                                                                  Ln: 6 Col: 4
```

Hence, it is always advised to implement exception handling as a good practice in your code.

Summary

The combination of Qt with Python provides the flexibility of Qt developers, develops GUI programs in a more robust language, and presents a rapid application development platform available on all major operating systems. We introduced to you the basics of PySide and its installation procedure on Windows, Linux, and Mac systems. We went on to create our first application, which introduced the main components of creating a GUI application and the event loop. We have concluded this chapter with an awareness on how to introduce exception handling as a best practice. Moving on, we are set to create some real-time applications in PySide.

2
Entering through Windows

The main part of any GUI program is to create windows and define functionalities around it. We will start exploring the ways to create windows and customize it in this chapter, and we will move on to create a real-life windows application in the next chapter.

The widget is the center of the user interface. It receives the user inputs from the mouse, keyboard, and other events of the window system, and paints a representation of itself on the screen. Every widget is rectangular, and sorted in a **Z-order**. Z-order is an ordering of displayed overlapping windows. The window with a higher Z-order will appear on top of windows with lower Z-orders. A widget is clipped by its parent and by the widgets in front of it. A widget that does not have a parent is called a *window* and is always independent. Usually, windows have a frame and a title bar at the least, but it is possible to create them without these by setting some windows flags. This chapter explains how to create simple windows using **QWidget** and also how to create some widely used widgets. The code snippets that are explained from this chapter onward will be based on **Object-Oriented Design principles**.

Creating a simple window

The `QWidget` is the base class for all the user interface classes. A widget can be a top-level widget or a child widget contained in a top-level or parent widget. Now, let's create a top-level window using `QWidget`. The constructor of the `QWidget` class takes two optional parameters, `parent` and `flags`. The `parent` parameter can be a `QWidget` object and the `flags` parameter can be a combination of `PySide.QtCore.Qt.WindowFlags`, as follows:

```
# Import required modules
import sys, time
```

```python
from PySide.QtGui import *
from PySide.QtCore import *

# Our main window class
class SampleWindow(QWidget):
    # Constructor function
    def __init__(self):
        super(SampleWindow,self).__init__()

        self.initGUI()


    def initGUI(self):
        self.setWindowTitle("Sample Window")
        self.setGeometry(300, 300, 200, 150)
        self.setMinimumHeight(100)
        self.setMinimumWidth(250)
        self.setMaximumHeight(200)
        self.setMaximumWidth(800)
        self.show()
        print("Sample Window show in the GUI\n")

if __name__ == '__main__':
    # Exception Handling
    try:
        myApp = QApplication(sys.argv)
        myWindow = SampleWindow()
        QCoreApplication.processEvents()
        time.sleep(3)
        myWindow.resize(300, 300)
        myWindow.setWindowTitle("Sample Window Resized")
        myWindow.repaint()
        myApp.exec_()
        sys.exit(0)
    except NameError:
        print("Name Error:", sys.exc_info()[1])
    except SystemExit:
        print("Closing Window...")
    except Exception:
        print (sys.exc_info()[1])
```

In this sample program, we create a window, set its minimum and maximum size, and repaint the window with different dimensions after a short period. If you look at the code closely, you will realize that the code follows the exception handling mechanism and object-oriented principles that were explained earlier.

The main idea in the earlier program is to introduce you to creating classes and objects, and work around them because programming in PySide indirectly implies programming using OO principles. PySide libraries follow the OO principles, and so do we. Our sample window is instantiated with the class that we declared for this purpose. The `SampleWindow` class is inherited from the `PySide.QtGui.QWidget` class. So, all the properties of `QWidget` can also be applied to our `SampleWindow` class. The `__init__` function is called the constructor that has to be shown when an object is instantiated while instantiating the object. In Python, object-oriented super function can be used to access inherited methods that have been overridden in a class. In sample code, we have to call the QtWidget initialization and hence, the `super(SampleWindow, self).__init__()` line. As the best practice, we have created function `initGUI` initialization in our sample window using the methods that are inherited from the `QWidget` class. The functions, `setMinimumHeight`, `setMinimumWidth`, set the window to minimum size and cannot be shrunk further. Similarly, the window cannot be extended beyond the maximum size specified by the functions, `setMaximumHeight` and `setMaximumWidth`, and we paint the window on the screen by calling the show function on the SampleWindow object.

Our `main` function is encapsulated in a `try`, `catch` block to deal with any unexpected exceptions that may occur. As explained in the previous chapter, every PySide application must create a main application object:

1. We will start with creating an object for the `QApplication` class. Then, we create an object for our custom defined `SampleWindow` class. At this point, the `__init__` function is called and all the properties that are defined for our sample window are set, and the window is displayed.

2. The lines that follow are just an example to show us that we can repaint the window with different dimensions at any point during the execution of the program. So, we hold on (sleep) for three seconds, resize the window, and repaint it on the screen.

3. Now, execute the code and have some fun. The event loop will be explained in Chapter ?. As of now, we should know that without `coreApplication.processEvents()`, we will not see the initial window with the title "Sample Window" and only see "Sample Window Resized". Go ahead and try to take a look at it yourself.

4. On executing the program, you will be shown a window, as shown in the following image. This window will get resized after three seconds.

Also, try to resize the window by dragging its corners. You may notice that the window cannot be shrunk or expanded beyond the minimum and maximum metrics set in our earlier code.

You may not initially see a window when executing this program on an XWindow-based system, such as Linux, because the main application loop has not been called yet. So, none of the objects have really been constructed and buffered out to the underlying XWindow system.

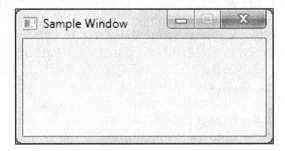

The following figure is the screenshot of the final output that you will see:

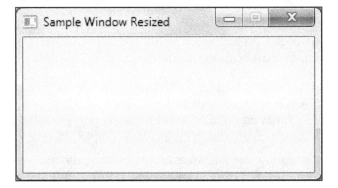

Creating the application icon

We created our sample window, and now we go on to customize it with some
features fitting our needs. For each customization, we add a new function under the
SampleWindow class in the previous program to define its properties, and we call this
our main function to apply these properties on the sample window. In this section,
we define an icon to be set on the window that we created. An icon is a small image
that is created to visually emphasize the purpose of the program. It is displayed
in the top-left corner of the application window. The same is also displayed in the
taskbar when the application is minimized. As a prerequisite for this program, you
may need an icon image with dimensions similar to the image that is used here (72
X 72). You can create your own image or download it from the book's website if you
wish to use the one used in this program:

```
# Import required modules
import sys, time
from PySide.QtGui import QApplication, QWidget, QIcon


# Our main window class
class SampleWindow(QWidget):
    # Constructor function
    def __init__(self):
        super(SampleWindow, self).__init__()

        self.initGUI()

    def initGUI(self):
        self.setWindowTitle("Icon Sample")
        self.setGeometry(300, 300, 200, 150)

    # Function to set Icon
        appIcon = QIcon('pyside_logo.png')
        self.setWindowIcon(appIcon)

        self.show()
```

```
if __name__ == '__main__':
    # Exception Handling
    try:
        myApp = QApplication(sys.argv)
        myWindow = SampleWindow()
        myApp.exec_()
        sys.exit(0)
    except NameError:
        print("Name Error:", sys.exc_info()[1])
    except SystemExit:
        print("Closing Window...")
    except Exception:
        print(sys.exc_info()[1])
```

The preceding program only requires the QApplication, QWidget, and QIcon import classes. As the best practice, we are loading only these required classes into our application in the import statement. Coming back to the preceding program, we included QIcon and setWindowIcon to set the application icon from the 'pyside_logo.png' file, and we call these functions from our initGUI function to set it.

As we are not specifying a file path, remember to place the image in the same location as the program. On executing this program, we will get the output as shown in the following screenshot:

As we have just seen the basics of setting an application icon, we will move on to explore more about the `PySide.QtGui.QIcon` class. This class provides a set of functions that provides scalable icons in different modes and states. Using this class, we can create various types of icons differing in their size and mode, namely, smaller, larger, active, and disabled from the set of `pixmaps` that is given. Such `pixmaps` are used by the Qt widgets to show an icon representing a particular action.

The `QIcon` class has the following different forms of constructors:

```
Qicon()
QIcon(QIconEngine * engine)
QIcon(QIconEngineV2 * engine)
QIcon(const QIcon & other)
QIcon(const QPixmap & pixmap)
QIcon(const QString & fileName)
```

The constructors in the preceding code are explained as follows:

* The first form constructs a null icon.

* The second and third form takes `PySide.QtGui.QIconEngine` as a parameter. These classes provide an abstract base class for the `QIcon` renderers. Each icon has a corresponding engine that has the responsibility to draw the icon with the requested size, mode, and state. The third `QIconEngineV2` extends `QiconEngine` with steaming capability and will be the standard engine starting from Qt4.8.

* The fourth form simply copies from the other `QIcon` object, and it is considered to be the fastest method of all.

* The fifth form constructs the icon from the `PySide.QtGui.QPixmap` class. This class is an off-screen image representation that can be used as a paint device. A `pixmap` can be easily displayed on the screen using `PySide.QtGui.QLabel` or one of the two button classes, `PySide.QtGui.QPushButton` or `PySide.QtGui.QToolButton`. `QLabel` has a `pixmap` property, whereas `QPushButton`/`QToolButton` has an icon property.

* The last form constructs an icon from the given filename. If the filename contains the relative path, it must be relative to the runtime working directory.

Icons are not only used for showing as application icon but also in various places as tool representation in the toolbars. Consider this, we are creating a toolbar in our application where we display icons to represent functionalities in pictorial form. A sample toolbar may appear like the one that is shown in the following screenshot:

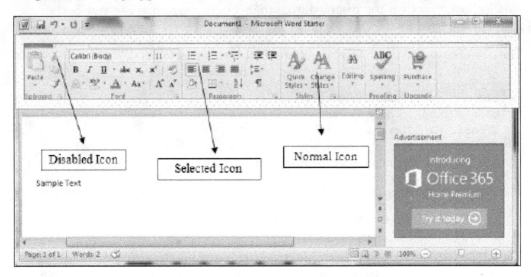

The QIcon class provides various modes to display the icon by the state it is defined as using the pixmap function applied to the QIcon class. The syntax of the pixmap function is PySide.QtGui.QIcon.pixmap(width, height[, mode=Normal[, state=Off]]). The parameters width and height represent the icon size. The modes can be any of the following four modes in the table depending on the action:

Constant	Description
QIcon.Normal	This displays the pixmap when the user is not interacting with the icon, but the functionality that is represented by the icon is available
QIcon.Disabled	This displays the pixmap when the functionality that is represented by the icon is not available
QIcon.Active	This displays the pixmap when the functionality that is represented by the icon is available and the user is interacting with the icon, for example, moving the mouse over it or clicking it
QIcon.Selected	This displays the pixmap when the item that is represented by the icon is selected

The `state` parameter can be used to describe the state for which `pixmap` is intended to be used. It can take any of the following two values in the table:

Constant	Description
QIcon.Off	This displays the `pixmap` when the widget is in an *off* state
QIcon.On	This displays the `pixmap` when the widget is in an *on* state

The following function will provide you with an example of various modes of icons that we create from setting the modes in the `pixmap` function. Add the following function from the previous program inside the `SampleWindow` class:

```
def setIconModes(self):
        myIcon1 = QIcon('pyside_logo.png')
        myLabel1 = QLabel('sample', self)
        pixmap1 = myIcon1.pixmap(50, 50, QIcon.Active, QIcon.On)
        myLabel1.setPixmap(pixmap1)
        myLabel1.show()

        myIcon2 = QIcon('pyside_logo.png')
        myLabel2 = QLabel('sample', self)
        pixmap2 = myIcon2.pixmap(50, 50, QIcon.Disabled, QIcon.Off)
        myLabel2.setPixmap(pixmap2)
        myLabel2.move(50, 0)
        myLabel2.show()

        myIcon3 = QIcon('pyside_logo.png')
        myLabel3 = QLabel('sample', self)
        pixmap3 = myIcon3.pixmap(50, 50, QIcon.Selected, QIcon.On)
        myLabel3.setPixmap(pixmap3)
        myLabel3.move(100, 0)
        myLabel3.show()
```

Now, add the following line in the `initGUI` function to call this function:

```
    . . .
        self.setWindowIcon(appIcon)
        self.setIconModes()
        self.show()
    . . .
```

You may have noted that a new QLabel widget was used in this program. The QLabel widget is used to provide a text or image display.

Running this program will output a window containing different modes of the same icon, as shown in the following screenshot:

Showing a tooltip

Our next customization is to show a tooltip for the different modes of icons that are shown. Tooltip is handy when you need to display some help text or information to the users. Displaying help text for the widgets that are used in the window is an integral part for any GUI application. We use the PySide.QtGui.QToolTip class to provide tooltips (also called balloon help) for any widget. The QToolTip class defines the properties of the tooltip, such as font, color, rich text display, and so on. As an example, the font properties can be set as follows:

```
QToolTip.setFont(QFont("Decorative", 8, QFont.Bold))
```

After setting the font, we set the tooltip to the widget by calling the setToolTip() function provided by the QWidget class:

```
myLabel1.setToolTip('Active Icon')
```

The QFont class specifies a font that has to be used to draw the text. Using the functions that are provided by this class, we can specify various attributes that we want our font to have. If the font type that we specify is not installed or available, Qt will try to use the closest match available. If a chosen font does not include all the characters that need to be displayed, QFont will try to find the characters in the nearest equivalent fonts. When a PySide.QtGui.QPainter draws a character from a font, the PySide.QtGui.Q font will report whether or not it has the character; if it does not, PySide.QtGui.Q Painter will draw an unfilled square.

Modify the previous program as shown in the following code snippet:

```
    . . .
def initGUI(self):
        self.setWindowTitle("Icon Sample")
        self.setGeometry(300, 300, 200, 150)
        QToolTip.setFont(QFont("Decorative", 8, QFont.Bold))
        self.setToolTip('Our Main Window')
    . . .


def setIconModes(self):
    . . .
        myLabel1.setPixmap(pixmap1)
        myLabel1.setToolTip('Active Icon')
        . . .
        myLabel2.move(50, 0)
        myLabel2.setToolTip('Disabled Icon')
        . . .
        myLabel3.move(100, 0)
        myLabel3.setToolTip('Selected Icon')
```

After making the changes, run the program and you can see that the tooltip text is displayed as and when you move over the icon and window. The sample output is displayed in the following screenshot:

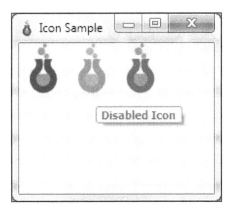

Adding a button

The next customization is to add a button to our application. The most common button that is used in any GUI is a push or command button. We push (click **on**) the button to command the computer to perform some action or answer a decision. Typical push buttons include: **OK, Apply, Cancel, Close, Yes, No**, and **Help**. Usually the **push** button is rectangular with some label on it. It can also have an optional icon associated with it. It is also possible to define a shortcut key combination to the button to which it responds on clicking the key combination.

The button emits a signal when it is activated by any external event, such as a mouse click or by pressing the spacebar, or by a keyboard shortcut. A widget may be associated with this key click event, which is executed on receiving this signal, and it is usually called a slot in *Qt*. We will learn more about signals and slots in the later chapters. As for now, be informed that a signal will connect to a slot on emission. There can also be other signals that are provided on a button, such as button pressed, button released, button checked, button down, button enabled, and so on. Apart from a **push** button, we also have other button types in Qt, such as QToolButton, QRadioButton, QCommandLinkButton, and QCheckBox, which will be discussed later.

QPushButton can be instantiated in three ways. It has three constructors with different signatures. They are as follows:

```
QPushButton(parent=None)
QPushButton(text, [parent=None])
QPushButton(icon, text, [parent=None])
```

The parent parameter can be any widget, while text is any string or a set of unicode characters, and icon is a valid QIcon object.

In this example program, we are going to add a button that will close the application when clicked. We define a button first and will call a function (*slot*) when clicked (*signal*):

```
def setButton(self):
    """ Function to add a quit button
    """
    myButton = QPushButton('Quit', self)
    myButton.move(50, 100)
    myButton.clicked.connect(self.quitApp)
```

Add the preceding function to the earlier example class and call the function from your `initGUI` conditional block before calling the `show()` function of `myWindow`. The important point here is the `clicked.connect()` call of the `myButton` object. The `clicked` event connects to the `myApp.quit()` slot, which quits the application. The slot can be replaced by an excerpt of code or a user-defined function, which performs a set of operations.

It is highly likely that the **quit** button may be pressed by mistake. If the application is quit without the user's confirmation there is a high chance of it being a mistake. So, we are going to display a confirmation message to the user on clicking the **quit** button. If the user wishes to quit, the application quits or the user can cancel it. The widely used widget for this purpose is `QMessageBox`. This is used to provide a modal dialog box to inform the user, or to ask the user a question and receive an answer. We will see more in detail about the `QMessageBox` in *Chapter 5, Dialogs and Widgets*. Here, for modularity and reusability, we created function `msgApp`, which takes an argument title and message and returns a **Yes** or **No**. Just create an instance of it and add it to our program. This provides reusability of this function across the application. This function is called by `quitApp` to display the confirmation message using the given title.

To do this, create these functions as follows:

```python
    #Function to Quit App that uses MsgApp
def quitApp(self):
    response = self.msgApp("Confirmation","This will quit the
application. Do you
    want to Continue?")

    if response == "Y":
        myApp.quit()
    else:
        pass


# Function to show Dialog box with provided Title and Message
def msgApp(self,title,msg):
    userInfo = QMessageBox.question(self,title,msg,
                            QMessageBox.Yes | QMessageBox.
No)
    if userInfo == QMessageBox.Yes:
        return "Y"
    if userInfo == QMessageBox.No:
        return "N"
```

Now, change the connect function in the `setButton` module to call the `quitApp` function on clicking the **quit** button:

```
myButton.clicked.connect(self.quitApp)
```

On executing the program and clicking on the quit button, you will get a confirmation message for which you can click on **Yes** or **No**:

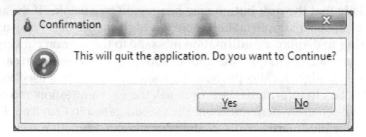

Clicking on **Yes** will quit the app and clicking on **No** will do nothing.

Centering the window on the screen

The windowed applications based on type and functionality get displayed in the center for main applications, top right for notifications, and as an icon in the status bar of the screen. It is best practice for any main GUI application to display the window centered on the screen. There are two advantages of doing this. The first is to get the attention of the user, and the other is to adjust to different display formats of the various monitor screens.

There is no straightforward method to center the window by calling a predefined function of some class. Therefore, we write our own method, called center, to position the window central to any screen. This method takes the object that it is calling and centers it with respect to the screen that it is displayed on:

```
def center(self):
    """ Function to center the application
    """
    qRect = self.frameGeometry()
    centerPoint = QDesktopWidget().availableGeometry().center()
    qRect.moveCenter(centerPoint)
    self.move(qRect.topLeft())
```

In order to do this, we first get the size and location of the window that we want to be centered. Then, we need to get the center point of the screen. Finally, we will move the window to the center of the screen. The `frameGeometry()` function will return a `PySide.QtCore.QRect` object that will hold the height, width, top, and left points of the window. The `QDesktopWidget().availableGeometry().center()` call will return the center point of the screen. The next two lines will move the window to the center point of the screen. Please remember to call this function before the `myWindow.show()` line to view the settings that are applied on your window.

About box

Our next customization to our application is to add the functionality to display an about box. An about box is a dialog box that displays credits and revision information about the application. It may also include the installed version and copyright information. The `QMessageBox` class provides a built-in function for this. It has the following signature:

```
PySide.QtGui.QMessageBox.about(parent, title, text)
```

The parent parameter takes any valid `QWidget` object. The title and text can be supplied with the Unicode parameter. The about box will have a single button labeled **OK**. To explain its working, we will now add a button named **About**, and on the click signal of this button, we call a slot which will display the **About box** to the user. The code for this is as follows:

```
    def setAboutButton(self):
        """ Function to set About Button
        """
        self.aboutButton = QPushButton("About", self)
        self.aboutButton.move(100, 100)
        self.aboutButton.clicked.connect(self.showAbout)

    def showAbout(self):
        """ Function to show About Box
        """
        QMessageBox.about(self.aboutButton, "About PySide",
                "PySide is a cross-platform tool for generating GUI
    Programs.")
```

Call this function from your `initGUI` block before the `self.show()` call. On execution, you will see a window with an added **About** button. On clicking this button, a separate dialog box is displayed with the heading and content text as given in the program. You can also note that the window also has the application icon displayed at the side by default. The sample output is displayed as follows for your reference:

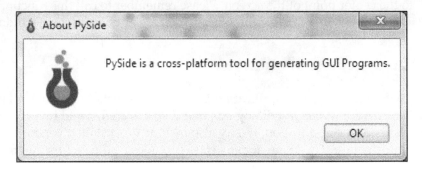

There is one more function that is provided by the `QMessage` class that may interest you. The `aboutQt` method is called, whose signature is given as follows:

```
PySide.QtGui.QMessageBox.aboutQt(parent[, title=""])
```

Calling this function will display a simple message box about `Qt`, with the given title and centered over parent. The message will display the version of the `Qt` that is currently used by the application. It is useful to display information about the platform that you are using in your program. As a learning exercise, try to implement this on your own and see what its output is.

Tracking time using timers

Most of the GUI applications are time bound, and it is extremely important to use timers to capture information about the program runtime and other similar tasks. You may also use timers to generate some event at specified time intervals, calculate the elapsed time for some action, implement a countdown timer, and so on. This section of the chapter covers how to create and use timers in our application, and we will develop a digital clock application explaining the concept of timers.

The classes that are used to create this application in Qt are `PySide.QtCore.QTimer` and `PySide.QtCore.QDateTime`. The `QTimer` class provides a high-level programming interface for timers. It provides repetitive and single-shot timers. Repetitive timers run continuously and restart at the expiry of one time slot. Single-shot timers will run exactly once and expire after one time slot. A timeout event will occur at the expiry of the given time slot. The timer can be started by issuing a start call to the `QTimer` object and can be stopped anywhere in between before the expiry of the time slot by issuing a stop signal:

```
QTimer.start(1000)
QTimer.stop()
```

The unit of the timer is in milliseconds. The accuracy of timers depends on the underlying operating system and hardware. Most platforms support a resolution of 1 millisecond, though the accuracy of the timer will not match this, and it is not guaranteed.

The `PySide.QtCore.QDateTime` class provides a calendar date and clock time function. It is a combination of the `PySide.QtCore.QDate` and `PySide.QtCore.QTime` classes. As with any other framework, the `QDateTime` class provides functions to compare datetimes and for manipulation of a datetime. It provides a full set operator to compare two `QDateTime` objects, where a smaller object means that it occured earlier and a larger object means that it occured later. The `QDateTime` can store datetimes both as local and as UTC. The `QDateTime.toUTC()` function can be applied on a `QDateTime` object to convert the local time to UTC. This class handles and is aware of daylight saving time:

```python
# Import required modules
import sys
from PySide.QtCore import QDateTime, QTimer, SIGNAL
from PySide.QtGui import QApplication, QWidget,
QLCDNumber,QDesktopWidget

class MyTimer(QWidget):
    """ Our Main Window class for Timer
    """
    def __init__(self):
        """ Constructor Function
        """
        super(MyTimer,self).__init__()
        self.initGUI()
```

```
    def initGUI(self):
        self.setWindowTitle('My Digital Clock')
        timer = QTimer(self)
        self.connect(timer, SIGNAL("timeout()"), self.updtTime)
        self.myTimeDisplay = QLCDNumber(self)
        self.myTimeDisplay.setSegmentStyle(QLCDNumber.Filled)
        self.myTimeDisplay.setDigitCount(8)
        self.myTimeDisplay.resize(500, 150)
        self.updtTime() # To Display the current time before call by
timer event. Otherwise it will start with 0
        self.center()
        timer.start(1000)
        self.show()

    def center(self):
        """
            Function to center the application
        """
        qRect = self.frameGeometry()
        centerPoint = QDesktopWidget().availableGeometry().center()
        qRect.moveCenter(centerPoint)
        self.move(qRect.topLeft())

    def updtTime(self):
        """ Function to update current time
        """
        currentTime = QDateTime.currentDateTime().toString('hh:mm:ss')
        self.myTimeDisplay.display(currentTime)

# Main Function
if __name__ == '__main__':
    # Exception Handling
    try:
        myApp = QApplication(sys.argv)
        myWindow = MyTimer()
        myApp.exec_()
        sys.exit(0)
    except NameError:
        print("Name Error:", sys.exc_info()[1])
    except SystemExit:
        print("Closing Window...")
    except Exception:
        print(sys.exc_info()[1])
```

The preceding program will display a digital clock on execution. To display the time with the precision in seconds, we start a timer that times out every second. On timeout of the timer, we call the `updtTime()` function, which will update the current time and display it on the screen. In order to display the time in the digital format, we used a special display in this program, which is different from the previous ones. The `PySide.QtGui.QLCDNumber` will display a number with LCD-like digits, which gives the appearance of a digital clock. The digits/numbers that can be shown with **LCDNumber** are **0/O, 1, 2, 3, 4, 5/S, 6, 7, 8, 9/g, minus, decimal point, A, B, C, D, E, F, h, H, L, o, P, r, u, U, Y, colon, degree sign** (which is specified as a single quote in the string) and **space**. `PySide.QtGui.QLCDNumber` substitutes spaces for illegal characters. Using this, we can just output the text/number in any size. The `setSegmentStyle()` function sets the style of the `QLCDNumber` that has to be displayed. It could take the following values, as displayed in the table:

Constant	Description
`QLCDNumber.Outline`	This gives us raised segments that are filled with the background color
`QLCDNumber.Filled`	This gives us raised segments that are filled with the windowText color
`QLCDNumber.Flat`	This gives us flat segments that are filled with the windowText color

One more thing to note here is that the `setDigitCount` function will set the number of digits to show on the display, which defaults to five.

Windows style

The PySide application can be executed under different platforms/flavors of operating systems. The GUI style of each flavor may vary in representing the application. If you require your application to look good on all platforms, you have to style your application in a way that is native to the operating system. Qt contains a set of style classes that emulate the styles of the different platforms. The abstract class that performs this in Qt is the PySide.QtGui.QStyle class. The classes that inherit this class and provide various style options are QCommonStyle, QWindowsStyle, QPlastiqueStyle, QCleanlooksStyle, QGtkStyle, QMotifStyle, and QCDEStyle. Qt's built-in widgets use QStyle to perform nearly all of their drawing, ensuring that they look exactly like the equivalent native widgets. As an example, the following screenshot contains the different representation of combobox in eight different styles under various OS platforms:

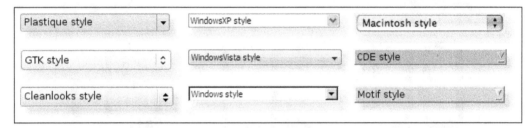

By default, Qt will choose the most appropriate style for the user's platform or desktop environment. The Windows style is the default style under flavors of Windows, **Plastique style** for Qt/X11 applications running under KDE, and **Cleanlooks** is the default under GNOME. These styles use gradients and antialiasing to provide a modern look and feel. The style of the entire application can be set using the QApplication.setStyle() function. It can also be specified by the user of the application, using the -style command-line option while running the program. The command-line option overrides the default style, as follows:

```
python myApp.py -style motif
```

The setStyle() function can also be applied to an individual widget. You can call QApplication.setStyle() any time, but by calling it before the constructor, you ensure that the user's preference, set using the -style command-line option, is respected.

Summary

In this chapter, we saw how to create Windows applications using widgets and dialogs. We also saw some customizations that were added to our application, and finished the chapter by creating a digital clock application. The knowledge gained in this chapter will help us in creating basic GUI applications using PySide and, more importantly, provide the foundation for any GUI application. We will start to explore creating main windowed applications, such as Notepad, and how to arrange visual components using different layouts in the coming chapters.

3
Main Windows and Layout Management

In the previous chapter, we saw how to create windows using widgets. Most of the **GUI** applications that we use today are main window-styled applications, which have a menu bar, toolbars, a status bar, a central widget, and optional dock widgets. Generally, an application will have a single main window and a collection of dialogs and widgets to serve the purpose of the application. A main window provides a framework to build an application's user interface. In this chapter, we shall discuss the creation of a main window application with its predefined components. We will also discuss layout management in a windowed application.

PySide provides a class, named `PySide.QtGui.QMainWindow`, that is derived from `QWidget` and its related classes for main-window management. `QMainWindow` has its own layout to which you can add toolbars, a menu bar, a status bar, dock widgets, and a central widget. The layout description of a main window is as shown in the following figure:

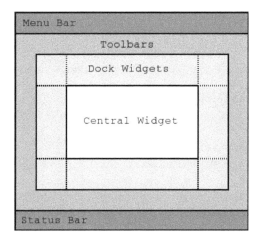

The central widget can be of any standard or custom widgets, say for example, QTextEdit or a QGraphicsView. Creating a main window without a central widget is not supported. Moving on, we will examine how to create a main window and will cover how to add its components one by one.

Creating the main window

As a first step, we will start with creating a main window by subclassing the QMainWindow class. The QMainWindow class has a constructor function that is similar to the QWidget class:

```
PySide.QtGui.QMainWindow([QWidget * parent = 0, Qt::WindowFlags flags
= 0)
```

The parent can be any valid QWidget object, and flags can be a valid combination of Qt.WindowFlags. The following code excerpt explains how to create a main window application at a very basic level:

```python
# Import required modules
import sys, time
from PySide.QtGui import QMainWindow,QApplication

# Our main window class
class MainWindow(QMainWindow):
    # Constructor function
    def __init__(self):
        super(MainWindow,self).__init__()
        self.initGUI()


    def initGUI(self):
        self.setWindowTitle("Main Window")
        self.setGeometry(300, 250, 400, 300)
        self.show()

if __name__ == '__main__':
    # Exception Handling
    try:

        myApp = QApplication(sys.argv)
        mainWindow = MainWindow()
        myApp.exec_()
        sys.exit(0)
```

```
except NameError:
    print("Name Error:", sys.exc_info()[1])
except SystemExit:
    print("Closing Window...")
except Exception:
    print(sys.exc_info()[1]
```

This will create a very minimal and basic main window with no other components, as shown in the following screenshot. In the forthcoming sections, we will see how to add these components in the main window.

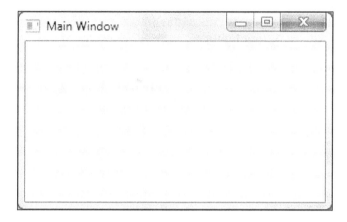

Status bar

A status bar is a horizontal information area that is usually found at the bottom of windows in a GUI. Its primary job is to display information about the current status of the window. A status bar can also be divided into sections, each showing different information to the users.

In PySide, a status bar can be added to the QMainWindow class by calling the QMainWindow.setStatusBar(statusbar) function. It takes the input parameter object of type PySide.QtGui.QStatusBar. The property of the status bar is defined by this class, and an object of this class is returned to set a status bar. Setting this parameter to 0 will remove the status bar from the main window. A status bar can show information that can fall into any of the following three categories:

- **Temporary**: This is mainly used to explain tooltip texts, menu entries, and so on. It temporarily occupies the enter status bar.

- **Normal**: This is used to display the current window information, page and line numbers, and so on. It is normally hidden by temporary messages and occupies a part of the status bar.

- **Permanent**: This usually occupies a small space, and it is used to indicate important mode information, the Caps Lock indicator, spell check information, line number in code editors, and so on.

At any give point of time, the current status bar object of type `QStatusBar` can be retrieved using the `QMainWindow.statusBar()` function. This object can then be used in a similar way to setting temporary messages on the status bar by calling the `QStatusBar.showMessage(text[, timeout=0])` function. If a timeout is set, the message will be cleared after the expiry of the specified time in milliseconds. If there is no timeout, you can clear the message by calling the `QStatusBar.clearMessage()` function.

To make this evident, we create a method called `CreateStatusBar()`, which has the following code snippet:

```
def CreateStatusBar(self):
    """ Function to create Status Bar
    """
    self.myStatusBar = QStatusBar()
    self.myStatusBar.showMessage('Ready', 2000)
    self.setStatusBar(self.myStatusBar)
```

Now, call this function from the `initGUI` function to set a status bar on the main window. On executing this code, we can see a status bar appearing on the main window that will expire after two seconds, which is the timeout that we have set. If you have left the timeout option or set it as `0`, the message will appear in the status bar until another message is called on to overwrite it or until we close the application. The output window will be as given in the following screenshot.

It is also possible to set a widget in the status bar in addition to the text messages. A widget, such as `QProgressBar`, can be added to the status bar to indicate the progress of a particular action on the main window. The `PySide.QtGui.QProgressBar` widget provides a horizontal or vertical progress bar. The progress bar is used to provide the user with an indication of the progress of an operation and to reassure them that the application is still running. We shall now take a look at a program that implements this. Make the changes to the previous program, explained as follows:

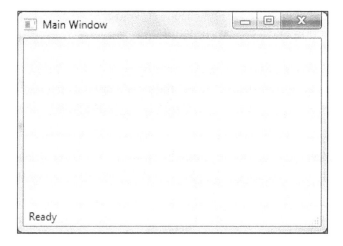

The setMinimum(minimum) and setMaximum(maximum) functions of PySide.QtGui. QProgressBar takes an integer value as the value to set the minimum and maximum possible step values. When you give it the current step value later, it will display the percentage of steps that have been completed. The percentage is calculated by dividing the progress, as follows:

```
[PySide.QtGui.QProgressBar.value() -PySide.QtGui.QProgressBar.
minimum()] /
[PySide.QtGui.QProgressBar.maximum() - PySide.QtGui.QProgressBar.
minimum()]
  def createProgressBar(self):
...
    self.progressBar = QProgressBar()
    self.progressBar.setMinimum(0)
    self.progressBar.setMaximum(100)
...
```

As explained, we will now add widgets to the status bar. For this purpose, we have created two widgets, namely, self.statusLabel and self.progressBar, of type QLabel and QProgressBar respectively. The following code creates the status bar and adds these widgets to it:

```
def CreateStatusBar(self):
  """ Function to create the status bar
  """
  self.myStatusBar = QStatusBar()
  self.myStatusBar.addWidget(self.statusLabel, 1)
  self.myStatusBar.addWidget(self.progressBar, 2)
  self.setStatusBar(self.myStatusBar)
```

The `PySide.QtGui.QStatusBar.addWidget` (QWidget * widget [, int
stretch=0]) function takes two arguments.

> The first mandatory argument is any valid `QWidget` object that has to
> be added on the status bar, and the second optional parameter is used to
> compute a suitable size for the given widget as the status bar grows and
> shrinks.

The number defines the ratio of the status bar that the widget can use. By setting the
progress bar's stretch factor to 2, we ensure that it takes two-thirds of the total area of
the status bar.

After adding the widgets to the status bar, we write the following function to show
its working state. This function will show the label as **Showing Progress** until the
progress bar at the right proceeds to completion. On progress reaching 100, the status
label changes to `Ready`:

```
def ShowProgress(self,progress):
  """ Function to show progress
  """
self.progressBar.setValue(progress)
        if progress == 100:
            self.statusLabel.setText('Ready')
            return
```

Now, modify the code in the `main` block, as shown in the following, and execute the
program. You can now see that the status bar has a working progress bar widget
along with a label:

```
. . . .
        mainWindow = MainWindow()
        mainWindow.CreateStatusBar()
        mainWindow.show()
        mainWindow.ShowProgress()
        myApp.exec_()
. . . .
```

Downloading the example code

You can download the example code files from your account at
`http://www.packtpub.com` for all the Packt Publishing books you
have purchased. If you purchased this book elsewhere, you can visit
`http://www.packtpub.com/support` and register to have the files
e-mailed directly to you.

After making the changes, execute the program and you will see an output window, as shown in the following screenshot:

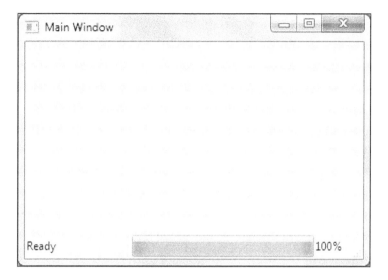

Menu bar

In the systems that use the command-line interface, the user may be presented with a list of commands that will be displayed as help text to the user. The users can then choose from the list to perform their desired action. In GUI systems, this is replaced with a set of text and symbols to represent choices. By clicking on the text/symbol, the user executes their desired action. This collection is called a menu.

A menu bar is a region of a screen or application that consists of a list of pull-down menu items. A common use of the menu bar is to provide convenient access to various operations, such as opening a new or an existing file, saving the file, printing options, manipulating data, providing help windows, closing the application, and so on. In this section, we introduce the concept of adding a menu bar to our application. Before that, we define the central widget of the application, which will aid the usage of menus.

The central widget

As we have seen earlier, the central area of the `QMainWindow` can be occupied by any kind of widget. This widget can be any of the following:

- A standard `Qt` widget, such as `QTextEdit` or `QGraphicsView`
- A custom widget created using primary widgets
- A plain `QWidget` with a layout manager, which acts as a parent for many other widgets
- Multiple widgets with a `QSplitter`, which arranges the widgets horizontally or vertically
- MDI area, which acts as a parent for other MDI windows

In our example, we use `QTextEdit` as the central widget. The `PySide.QtGui.QTextEdit` class provides a widget that is used to edit and display both plain and rich text formats and also displays images, lists, and tables. `QTextEdit` is an advanced **WYSIWYG** viewer/editor using HTML style tags. The rich text support in `Qt` is designed to provide a fast, portable, and efficient way to add reasonable online help facilities to applications, and to provide a basis for rich text editors. The `QTextEdit` can be used as both a display widget and an editor. For our purposes, we use it as an editor.

The following piece of code sets the `QTextEdit` as the central widget. On calling this function from the `initGUI` function, a text editor will be set at the central space of our application. The output is shown in the screenshot after the information box containing the code excerpt:

```
def SetupComponents(self):
    """ Setting the central widget
        """
        textEdit = QTextEdit()
        self.setCentralWidget(textEdit)
```

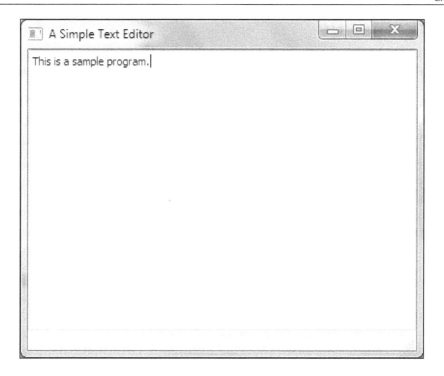

Adding a menu bar

We will now add the menu bar to our application. We use the PySide.QtGui.
QMenuBar class to create a menu bar. This class provides a horizontal menu bar to
which the menu items can be added. You don't have to set a layout for the menu bar.
Different platforms use different layouts for the menu bar. In a Windows system,
the menu bar is usually anchored at the top of a window under the title bar. In the
Macintosh system, the menu bar is usually anchored at the top of the screen. Linux
systems have both these display formats depending on the GUI style. QMenuBar
automatically sets its own geometry to the top of the parent widget and changes it
appropriately whenever the parent is resized.

In the main window style applications, we use the PySide.QtGui.QMainWindow.
menuBar() function to create a menu bar. This function will return an empty menu
bar, which has QMainWindow as its parent. In the Mac application, if you want all
to share a single common menu bar, use PySide.QtGui.QMenuBar and don't use
a function to create it, because the menu bar that is created this way will have
QMainWindow as its parent with no parent by directly instantiating the QMenuBar
class. The menu bar can also be set in the main window using the PySide.QtGui.
QMainWindow.setMenuBar(menubar) function, which takes a menu bar object as its
parameter.

Adding menus

Once the menu bar is set, a menu list can be added to it. The `PySide.QtGui.QMenu` class provides a menu widget for use in menu bars, context menus, and other pop-up menus. A menu widget is a selection menu, which can be either a pull-down menu in a menu bar or it can be a context menu. Pull-down menus are shown by the menu bar when the user clicks on the respective item or presses the specified shortcut key. Context menus are invoked by some special keyboard key or by right-clicking on it.

In the menu bar, we add menus with the `QMenuBar.addMenu(menu)` function. For the example application, we add three menus namely, `File`, `Edit`, and `About`. Inside each of these menus, we create two actions, each that connects to a specified slot. As defined, a menu consists of a list of action items when triggered by a click or a keyboard shortcut key combination. The `PySide.QtGui.QAction` class provides an abstract user interface action that can be inserted into widgets. Actions are common for a combination of menu items, toolbars, and keyboard shortcuts. So, we create an action and attach it to different components that are expected to perform the same functionality. Usually, when an action is created, it should be added to the relevant menu and toolbar, and then connected to the slot that will perform the action. Actions are added to the menus with the `QMenu.addAction()`, `QMenu.addActions()`, and `QMenu.insertAction()` functions. An action is rendered vertically under the menu, and can have a text label, an optional icon drawn on the left, and a shortcut key sequence.

The following example demonstrates the creation of the menu bar in the main window application. This program is a shortened version of what we will be developing as a fully working **Simple Text Editor** application at the end of this chapter:

```
# Import required modules
import sys
from PySide.QtGui import QApplication, QMainWindow, QStatusBar, \
QTextEdit, \
    QAction, QIcon, QKeySequence

class MainWindow(QMainWindow):
  """ Our Main Window class
  """

  def __init__(self):
    """ Constructor Function
    """
    super(MainWindow, self).__init__()
    self.initGUI()
```

```
def initGUI(self):
    self.setWindowTitle("A Simple Text Editor")
    self.setWindowIcon(QIcon('appicon.png'))
    self.setGeometry(300, 250, 400, 300)
    self.SetupComponents()
    self.show()

def SetupComponents(self):
    """ Function to setup status bar, central widget, menu bar
    """
    self.myStatusBar = QStatusBar()
    self.setStatusBar(self.myStatusBar)
    self.myStatusBar.showMessage('Ready', 10000)
    self.textEdit = QTextEdit()
    self.setCentralWidget(self.textEdit)
    self.CreateActions()
    self.CreateMenus()
    self.fileMenu.addAction(self.newAction)
    self.fileMenu.addSeparator()
    self.fileMenu.addAction(self.exitAction)
    self.editMenu.addAction(self.copyAction)
    self.fileMenu.addSeparator()
    self.editMenu.addAction(self.pasteAction)
    self.helpMenu.addAction(self.aboutAction)


# Slots called when the menu actions are triggered
def newFile(self):
  self.textEdit.setText('')

def exitFile(self):
  self.close()

def aboutHelp(self):
  QMessageBox.about(self, "About Simple Text Editor",
      "This example demonstrates the use "
      "of Menu Bar")

def CreateActions(self):
  """ Function to create actions for menus
  """
  self.newAction = QAction( QIcon('new.png'), '&New',
            self, shortcut=QKeySequence.New,
            statusTip="Create a New File",
```

```
                        triggered=self.newFile)
        self.exitAction = QAction( QIcon('exit.png'), 'E&xit',
                        self, shortcut="Ctrl+Q",
                        statusTip="Exit the Application",
                        triggered=self.exitFile)
        self.copyAction = QAction( QIcon('copy.png'), 'C&opy',
                        self, shortcut="Ctrl+C",
                        statusTip="Copy",
                        triggered=self.textEdit.copy)
        self.pasteAction = QAction( QIcon('paste.png'), '&Paste',
                        self, shortcut="Ctrl+V",
                        statusTip="Paste",
                        triggered=self.textEdit.paste)
        self.aboutAction = QAction( QIcon('about.png'), 'A&bout',
                        self, statusTip="Displays info about text editor",
                        triggered=self.aboutHelp)


    # Actual menu bar item creation
    def CreateMenus(self):
        """ Function to create actual menu bar
        """
        self.fileMenu = self.menuBar().addMenu("&File")
        self.editMenu = self.menuBar().addMenu("&Edit")
        self.helpMenu = self.menuBar().addMenu("&Help")


if __name__ == '__main__':
    # Exception Handling
    try:
        #QApplication.setStyle('plastique')
        myApp = QApplication(sys.argv)
        mainWindow = MainWindow()
        myApp.exec_()
        sys.exit(0)
    except NameError:
        print("Name Error:", sys.exc_info()[1])
    except SystemExit:
        print("Closing Window...")
    except Exception:
        print(sys.exc_info()[1])
```

In the preceding example, the actions are created in the `CreateActions()` function. Each of the menu items is created as a separate action:

```
self.newAction = QAction( QIcon('new.png'), '&New',
  self, shortcut=QKeySequence.New,
  statusTip="Create a New File",
  triggered=self.newFile)
```

The **New** item under the **File** menu has the action instantiated as the preceding code snippet. Its parameters are explained as follows:

- The first parameter is the **Icon** that will be displayed to the left of the menu item.

- The next parameter is the name that has to be displayed. The `&` character represents that the letter followed by it should be underlined, and it can be accessed by pressing the **Alt +** <letter> combination as in many other window applications.

- The third parameter implies the parent, which is the main window here.

- The fourth and fifth keyword parameters represent the shortcut key combination for easy access of the menu item and the status tip that has to be displayed on highlighting the menu item, respectively. The shortcut key can be either a predefined combination by the `PySide.QtGui.QKeySequence` class or a valid combination as given by the user. The `PySide.QtGui.QKeySequence` class encapsulates a key sequence that is used by shortcuts. It defines a combination of keys that can be used by different operating system platforms.

- The last parameter defines the slot that has to be called when the menu item is triggered, which can be a logical group of code executing the desired functionality. We define the other actions similar to this.

Once the actions are created, we add these actions to the menu items. The top-level menu bar is created in the `CreateMenus()` function and the actions of the menu items are added, as follows:

```
self.fileMenu.addAction(self.newAction)
```

The menu items can be grouped by adding a separator between the items, which is done as given in the following code line:

```
self.fileMenu.addSeparator()
```

Execute the program and witness how menus work.

Toolbar

A toolbar is a panel of icons that is associated with actions that are available for easy access of menus. In PySide, the toolbars are implemented in the `PySide.QtGui.QToolBar` class. The toolbar is added to the main window with the `addToolBar()` function. The toolbar is initially positioned at the top of the window below the menu bar. This can be adjusted with the `QToolBar.setAllowedAreas()` function. The tool bar can be set as movable or immovable by setting it with the `QToolBar.setMovable()` function. The style and size of the icons can be defined by the underlying platform, which can also be controlled. When it is resized in a way that is too small to hold all the icons, an **Extension** button will appear, which on clicking expands to all items.

Toolbar buttons are added using actions as seen in the menu bar creation in the previous section; we can even use the same actions. The following example demonstrates the creation of a toolbar and its usage:

```
def CreateToolBar(self):
    """ Function to create tool bar
    """
    self.mainToolBar = self.addToolBar('Main')
```

The actions can be added as follows. These lines should be appended in the `SetupComponents()` function after invoking the `CreateToolBar()` module in our previous example:

```
self.mainToolBar.addAction(self.newAction)
self.mainToolBar.addSeparator()
self.mainToolBar.addAction(self.copyAction)
self.mainToolBar.addAction(self.pasteAction)
```

Thus, we have seen how to add the discussed components in the main window.

Layout management

A layout can be defined as the sizing, spacing, and placement of content within a GUI window. It defines the visual structure of a user interface. Effective layout management will please users by assisting them in quickly locating what the users want most from the application, and also helps in making out the differences between a good informative design and confusing, puzzling designs for the application. Therefore, management of layout in a window-style application is a crucial success factor for any GUI application. A good layout must have a priority focus, smooth flow, logical grouping, relative emphasis, and coordinated alignment.

In PySide, we use two approaches to layout management. They are as follows:

- **Absolute positioning**: This is a crude way of setting the layout manually for each widget by giving them their position and size

- **Layout containers**: This is a way to handle the automatic positioning and resizing of widgets by the layout management classes used in Qt

Absolute positioning

Absolute positioning is the most crude and naive form of arranging widgets in the window. This is achieved by giving a hard-wired position and size to all the widgets in the window. Usually, we use the widget's move(x, y) function where x and y are the horizontal and vertical distance, respectively, from the top left corner of the form to the top left corner of the widget. We have already seen this method of layout positioning in our previous chapters when positioning the About and Quit buttons.

This method of layout management is highly discouraged and not effective due to the following disadvantages:

- Calculating the size and position for each widget manually is a really cumbersome task

- Resizing the window changes the layout

- It does not respond to style changes

- Internationalization and font changes become very difficult as the label text may overflow or underflow

- It may appear completely different in different resolutions

Therefore, it is highly advised to use the layout containers for layout management. We have already seen examples for this type of layout management.

Layout containers

All widgets can use layouts to manage their children. If these are used in a proper way, the following functions are achieved:

- Sensible default size for windows

- Positioning of child widgets

- Resize handling

- Automatic updates when content changes, including font size, hiding, removal of widgets, and so on

The container class overcomes all the disadvantages that were discussed in absolute positioning and is the most widely used layout management system. Containers are more flexible and adjust the layout in accordance with the style of the different platforms. We will look into the commonly used layout containers inherited from the `PySide.QtGui.QLayout` class:

- `QBoxLayout`: This lines up widgets horizontally or vertically, as follows:
    - `QHBoxLayout`: This lines up widgets horizontally
    - `QVBoxLayout`: This lines up widgets vertically
- `QGridLayout`: This lays out widgets in a grid
- `QFormLayout`: This manages the form of input widgets and their label
- `QStackedLayout`: This is a stack of widgets where only one widget is visible at a time

We will discuss each of them in slight detail.

QBoxLayout

The `PySide.QtGui.QBoxLayout` class takes the space it gets, divides it up into a row of boxes, and makes each managed widget fill one box. The orientation or direction of the box layout can be either vertical (column-wise) or horizontal (row-wise). The direction can take any one of the following values:

- `QBoxLayout.LeftToRight`: This takes the horizontal direction from left to right
- `QBoxLayout.RightToLeft`: This takes the horizontal direction from right to left
- `QBoxLayout.TopToBottom`: This takes the vertical direction from top to bottom
- `QBoxLayout.BottomToTop`: This takes the vertical direction from bottom to top

Each of the filled widgets will get its minimum size at the least and its maximum size at the most. The extra space is shared between the widgets according to their stretch factor. The `QBoxLayout` class can be attached to any of the parent layouts because it is not the top-level layout.

The widgets can be added to the `QBoxLayout` function using the following four functions:

- `QBoxLayout.addWidget()`: This helps add widgets
- `QBoxLayout.addSpacing()`: This creates an empty box to add spacing
- `QBoxLayout.addStretch()`: This creates an empty stretchable box
- `QBoxLayout.addLayout()`: This adds a box with another layout and defines its stretch factor

The add functions can be replaced with insert functions, for example, `QBoxLayout.insertWidget()` to insert a box at a specified position in the layout.

This class also includes two margins. The `Pyside.QtGui.QLayout.setContentsMargins()` function sets the width of the outer border on each side of the widget, and `PySide.QtGui.QBoxLayout.setSpacing()` sets the width between the neighboring boxes. The default margin spaces differ by the application style.

The most convenient and easy way to use the `QBoxLayout` class is to instantiate one of its inherited classes, `QVBoxLayout` and `QHBoxLayout`, for vertical and horizontal direction layout, respectively. The following programs will explain the usage of `QVBoxLayout` and `QHBoxLayout`.

QHBoxLayout

An example of the horizontal layout is as follows:

```
class MainWindow(QWidget):
  """ Our Main Window class
  """
  def __init__(self):
    """ Constructor Function
    """
    super(MainWindow,self).__init__()
    self.initGUI()
```

```
def initGUI(self):
    self.setWindowTitle("Horizontal Layout")
    self.setGeometry(300, 250, 400, 300)
    self.SetLayout()
    self.show()


def SetLayout(self):
    """ Function to add buttons and set the layout
    """
    horizontalLayout = QHBoxLayout(self)
    hButton1 = QPushButton('Button 1', self)
    hButton2 = QPushButton('Button 2', self)
    hButton3 = QPushButton('Button 3', self)
    hButton4 = QPushButton('Button 4', self)
    horizontalLayout.addWidget(hButton1)
    horizontalLayout.addWidget(hButton2)
    horizontalLayout.addWidget(hButton3)
    horizontalLayout.addWidget(hButton4)

    self.setLayout(horizontalLayout)
```

QVBoxLayout

An example of the vertical layout is as follows:

```
def SetLayout(self):
    verticalLayout = QVBoxLayout(self)
    vButton1 = QPushButton('Button 1', self)
    vButton2 = QPushButton('Button 2', self)
    vButton3 = QPushButton('Button 3', self)
    vButton4 = QPushButton('Button 4', self)

    verticalLayout.addWidget(vButton1)
    verticalLayout.addWidget(vButton2)
    verticalLayout.addStretch()
    verticalLayout.addWidget(vButton3)
    verticalLayout.addWidget(vButton4)

    self.setLayout(verticalLayout)
```

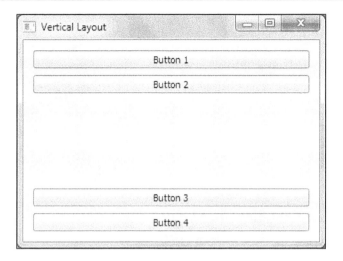

QGridLayout

The `PySide.QtGui.QGridLayout` class takes the space that is available to it, divides it up into rows and columns, and puts each widget that it manages into the next available cell. Similar to HTML tables, each row/column has a minimum width and a stretch factor. The widgets are added into the grid layout using the `addWidget()` function and the layout puts it into the correct cell. It is also possible for a widget to span across multiple rows/columns. The `addItem()` and `addLayout()` methods can also be used to insert widgets or other layouts into it.

The grid layout also includes two margins, as discussed in the box layout. An example program for the usage of grid layout is as follows:

```
def SetLayout(self):
    gridLayout = QGridLayout(self)
    gButton1 = QPushButton('Button 1', self)
    gButton2 = QPushButton('Button 2', self)
    gButton3 = QPushButton('Button 3', self)
    gButton4 = QPushButton('Button 4', self)
    gButton5 = QPushButton('Button 5', self)
    gridLayout.addWidget(gButton1, 0, 0)
    gridLayout.addWidget(gButton2, 0, 1)
    gridLayout.addWidget(gButton3, 1, 0, 1, 2)
    gridLayout.addWidget(gButton4, 2, 0)
    gridLayout.addWidget(gButton5, 2, 1)
  self.setLayout(gridLayout)
```

QFormLayout

The `PySide.QtGui.QFormLayout` class is a higher-level alternative to the basic forms of layout classes, which lays out its widgets in a two-column form. Usually, the left column consists of `label`, and the right column consists of the `field` widgets, such as line editors, combo box, spin box, and so on.

The form layout can be achieved through the grid layout, but using it directly on the form-like widgets has the following advantages:

- Adherence to different platforms' look and feel
- Support to wrap long rows, using *RowWrapPolicy* control
- API to create *label-field* pairs
- Support to expand fields using *FieldGrowthPolicy* control

The spacing between the rows of forms can be set using the `setHorizontalSpacing()` and `setVerticalSpacing()` functions of this class. An example of the form layout is as follows:

```
def SetLayout(self):
    formLayout = QFormLayout(self)
    labelUsername = QLabel("Username")
    txtUsername = QLineEdit()
    labelPassword = QLabel("Password")
    txtPassword = QLineEdit()
    formLayout.addRow(labelUsername, txtUsername)
    formLayout.addRow(labelPassword, txtPassword)
    self.setLayout(formLayout)
```

QStackedLayout

The `PySide.QtGui.QStackedLayout` class lays out a set of child widgets, and it shows them only one at a time, hiding the others from the user. The layout can be initially populated with a number of child widgets, and later on, any one of them can be selected to be shown to the user depending on the choice in window. There is no intrinsic way given by the layout itself for the users to select a widget from the available child widgets. This is achieved through using either `QComboBox` or `QListWidget` widgets. On populating the layout, the child widgets are added to an internal list, and the index is returned by the layout to select child widgets. The widgets can be inserted and removed using the `insertWidget()` and `removeWidget()` functions respectively.

The implementation of the stack layout is left as an exercise for you. The sample program can be found in the code samples that come along with this book.

SDI and MDI

In many GUI applications, we will arrive at a situation where we need to open more than one document at a time to process them. We will want to design our application to handle this. This can be achieved by either of two approaches, namely, SDI and MDI. A **Single Document Interface (SDI)** application implements this by creating separate windows for each of the documents. This is done by creating a window subclass that handles everything by itself, including loading, saving, cleaning up, and so on. Each of the documents will be a clone of the main window having a separate menu bar, toolbar, and status bar on its own. Each of the main window instances must be able to act independently. However, there are some disadvantages to this approach. This approach consumes a lot of resources and it would be very inconvenient to open many windows at a time and keep track of them.

The second approach is to use a **Multiple Document Interface (MDI)** application where the central widget is instantiated with multiple instances. All these widgets will be interrelated within the main window and share the common menu bar, toolbar, and other components. MDI applications will use lesser resources compared with SDI applications. The MDI applications are provided with an extra menu to manage between windows because shifting between them is not controlled by the underlying operating system. We will discuss more about SDI and MDI, and their implementation in *Chapter 5, Dialogs and Widgets*.

A simple text editor

The following is the implementation of a simple text editor that is extended from the previous examples in its building version. This code contains some new features, such as QFontDialog, QFileDialog, and so on, which are discussed in *Chapter 5, Dialogs and Widgets*. Otherwise, the following code is self explanatory:

```
# Import required modules
import sys, time
from PySide.QtGui import *


# Our main window class
class MainWindow(QMainWindow):

    # Constructor function
    def __init__(self, fileName=None):
        super(MainWindow,self).__init__()
        self.initGUI()
```

```python
def initGUI(self):
    self.setWindowTitle("A Simple Text Editor")
    self.setWindowIcon(QIcon('appicon.png'))
    self.setGeometry(100, 100, 800, 600)

    self.textEdit = QTextEdit()
    self.setCentralWidget(self.textEdit)
    self.fileName = None

    self.filters = "Text files (*.txt)"
    self.SetupComponents()
    self.show()

# Function to setup status bar, central widget, menu bar, tool bar
def SetupComponents(self):
    self.myStatusBar = QStatusBar()
    self.setStatusBar(self.myStatusBar)
    self.myStatusBar.showMessage('Ready', 10000)

    self.CreateActions()
    self.CreateMenus()
    self.CreateToolBar()
    self.fileMenu.addAction(self.newAction)
    self.fileMenu.addAction(self.openAction)
    self.fileMenu.addAction(self.saveAction)
    self.fileMenu.addSeparator()
    self.fileMenu.addAction(self.exitAction)
    self.editMenu.addAction(self.cutAction)
    self.editMenu.addAction(self.copyAction)
    self.editMenu.addAction(self.pasteAction)
    self.editMenu.addSeparator()
    self.editMenu.addAction(self.undoAction)
    self.editMenu.addAction(self.redoAction)
    self.editMenu.addSeparator()
    self.editMenu.addAction(self.selectAllAction)
    self.formatMenu.addAction(self.fontAction)
    self.helpMenu.addAction(self.aboutAction)
    self.helpMenu.addSeparator()
    self.helpMenu.addAction(self.aboutQtAction)
    self.mainToolBar.addAction(self.newAction)
    self.mainToolBar.addAction(self.openAction)
    self.mainToolBar.addAction(self.saveAction)
    self.mainToolBar.addSeparator()
```

```
        self.mainToolBar.addAction(self.cutAction)
        self.mainToolBar.addAction(self.copyAction)
        self.mainToolBar.addAction(self.pasteAction)
        self.mainToolBar.addSeparator()
        self.mainToolBar.addAction(self.undoAction)
        self.mainToolBar.addAction(self.redoAction)


    # Slots called when the menu actions are triggered
    def newFile(self):
        response = self.msgApp("Confirmation","Do you like to save the
current file?")
        if response == "Y":
            self.saveFile()

        self.textEdit.setText('')
        self.fileName = None

    def openFile(self):
        response = self.msgApp("Confirmation","Do you like to save the
current file?")
        if response == "Y":
            self.saveFile()

        self.fileName, self.filterName = QFileDialog.
getOpenFileName(self)
        self.textEdit.setText(open(self.fileName).read())

    def saveFile(self):
        if self.fileName == None or self.fileName == '':
            self.fileName, self.filterName = QFileDialog.
getSaveFileName(self, filter=self.filters)
        if(self.fileName != ''):
            file = open(self.fileName, 'w')
            file.write(self.textEdit.toPlainText())
            self.statusBar().showMessage("File saved", 2000)

    def exitFile(self):
        response = self.msgApp("Confirmation","This will quit the
application. Do you want to Continue?")
        if response == "Y":
            myApp.quit()
        else:
```

```
                    pass

        # Function to show Diaglog box with provided Title and Message
        def msgApp(self,title,msg):
            userInfo = QMessageBox.question(self,title,msg,
                                    QMessageBox.Yes | QMessageBox.
No)
            if userInfo == QMessageBox.Yes:
                return "Y"
            if userInfo == QMessageBox.No:
                return "N"
            self.close()


        def fontChange(self):
            (font, ok) = QFontDialog.getFont(QFont("Helvetica [Cronyx]",
10), self)
            if ok:
                self.textEdit.setCurrentFont(font)


        def aboutHelp(self):
            QMessageBox.about(self, "About Simple Text Editor",
                    "A Simple Text Editor where you can edit and save
files")


        # Function to create actions for menus
        def CreateActions(self):
            self.newAction = QAction( QIcon('new.png'), '&New',
                                self, shortcut=QKeySequence.New,
                                statusTip="Create a New File",
                                triggered=self.newFile)
            self.openAction = QAction( QIcon('open.png'), 'O&pen',
                                self, shortcut=QKeySequence.Open,
                                statusTip="Open an existing file",
                                triggered=self.openFile)
            self.saveAction = QAction( QIcon('save.png'), '&Save',
                                self, shortcut=QKeySequence.Save,
                                statusTip="Save the current file to
disk",
                                triggered=self.saveFile)
            self.exitAction = QAction( QIcon('exit.png'), 'E&xit',
                                self, shortcut="Ctrl+Q",
                                statusTip="Exit the Application",
                                triggered=self.exitFile)
            self.cutAction = QAction( QIcon('cut.png'), 'C&ut',
```

```
                                        self, shortcut=QKeySequence.Cut,
                                        statusTip="Cut the current
selection to clipboard",
                                        triggered=self.textEdit.cut)
        self.copyAction = QAction( QIcon('copy.png'), 'C&opy',
                                        self, shortcut=QKeySequence.Copy,
                                        statusTip="Copy the current
selection to clipboard",
                                        triggered=self.textEdit.copy)
        self.pasteAction = QAction( QIcon('paste.png'), '&Paste',
                                         self, shortcut=QKeySequence.Paste,
                                        statusTip="Paste the clipboard's
content in current location",
                                        triggered=self.textEdit.paste)
        self.selectAllAction = QAction( QIcon('selectAll.png'),
'Select All',
                                          self, statusTip="Select All",
                                        triggered=self.textEdit.selectAll)
        self.redoAction = QAction( QIcon('redo.png'),'Redo', self,
                                        shortcut=QKeySequence.Redo,
                                        statusTip="Redo previous action",
                                        triggered=self.textEdit.redo)
        self.undoAction = QAction( QIcon('undo.png'),'Undo', self,
                                        shortcut=QKeySequence.Undo,
                                        statusTip="Undo previous action",
                                        triggered=self.textEdit.undo)
        self.fontAction = QAction( 'F&ont', self,
                                        statusTip = "Modify font
properties",
                                        triggered = self.fontChange)
        self.aboutAction = QAction( QIcon('about.png'), 'A&bout',
                                         self, statusTip="Displays info
about text editor",
                                        triggered=self.aboutHelp)
        self.aboutQtAction = QAction("About &Qt", self,
                                       statusTip="Show the Qt library's About
box",
                                       triggered=qApp.aboutQt)
    # Actual menu bar item creation
    def CreateMenus(self):
        self.fileMenu = self.menuBar().addMenu("&File")
        self.editMenu = self.menuBar().addMenu("&Edit")
        self.formatMenu = self.menuBar().addMenu("F&ormat")
        self.helpMenu = self.menuBar().addMenu("&Help")
```

```
def CreateToolBar(self):
    self.mainToolBar = self.addToolBar('Main')


if __name__ == '__main__':
    # Exception Handling
    try:
        myApp = QApplication(sys.argv)
        mainWindow = MainWindow()
        myApp.exec_()
        sys.exit(0)
    except NameError:
        print("Name Error:", sys.exc_info()[1])
    except SystemExit:
        print("Closing Window...")
    except Exception:
        print(sys.exc_info()[1])
```

The sample output of the preceding program is given in the following screenshot:

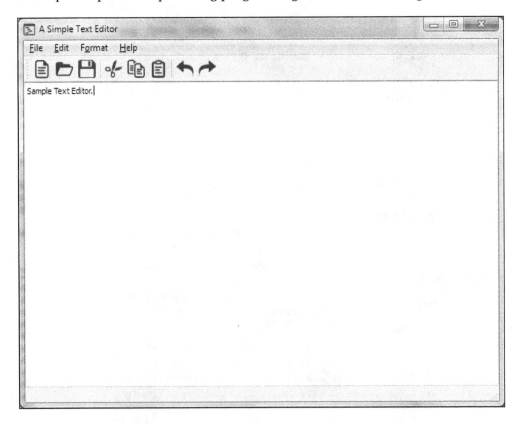

The preceding example is a very simple text editor performing some basic functions. We will build upon this example in the coming chapters, as and when we discuss some new features.

Summary

In this chapter, we saw how to create the most widely used main window-styled applications. We also learned about the layout management in applications. We completed the chapter with a real-time text editor example. We will build on the text editor example. In the next chapter, we will learn how interactive applications can be built using events and signals concepts.

4
Events and Signals

In the chapters that we saw so far, we tried out various implementations of readily available functions to build a base GUI by extending the Qt objects without handling custom events. In this chapter, we will look into some of the internal implementations of working concepts of these functions in the context of events and signals. Qt being an event-driven UI toolkit, events and event delivery play an important role in the Qt architecture. We will start this chapter by discussing events and signals, their implementation, and will go on to discuss handling drag and drop events, and drawing functionalities.

Event management

An event, in general, is some change in state in discrete time that is induced by external or internal actions. An event action in Qt is an object that is inherited from the abstract `QEvent` class, which is a notification of something significant that has happened. Events become more useful in creating custom widgets on our own. An event can happen either within an application or as a result of an outside activity that the application needs to know about. When an event occurs, Qt creates an event object and notifies the instance of a `QObject` class or one of its subclasses through the `event()` function. Events can be generated from both inside and outside the application. For instance, the `QKeyEvent` and `QMouseEvent` objects represent some kind of keyboard and mouse interaction, and they come from the window manager. The `QTimerEvent` objects are sent to `QObject` when one of its timers fires, and they usually come from the operating system. The `QChildEvent` objects are sent to `QObject` when a child is added or removed, and they come from inside of your Qt application.

The users of PySide usually get confused with events and signals. Events and signals are two parallel mechanisms that are used to accomplish the same thing. As a general difference, signals are useful when using a widget, whereas events are useful when implementing the widget. For example, when we are using a widget, such as QPushButton, we are more interested in its clicked() signal than in the low-level mouse press or key press events that caused the signal to be emitted. But if we are implementing the QPushButton class to validate on mouse press, we are more interested in the implementation of code for mouse press or key down events. Hence, events are generated by an external entity, such as keyboard, mouse, and so on, and when we want to get notified, signals are used. Don't worry if you don't get it, we will go through this in the next sections.

Event loop

All the events in Qt will go through an event loop. One of the main key concepts to be noted here is that the events are not delivered as soon as they are generated; instead, they're queued up in an event queue and processed later one by one. The event dispatcher will loop through this queue and dispatch these events to the target QObject, and hence, it is called an **event loop**. Qt's main event loop dispatcher, QApplication.exec(), will fetch the native window system events from the event queue and will process them, convert them into the QEvent objects, and send them to their respective target QObject.

A simple event loop can be explained as described in the following pseudo-code:

```
while(application_is_active)
{
  while(event_exists_in_event_queue)
    process_next_event();

  wait_for_more_events();
}
```

The Qt's main event loop starts with the QApplication::exec() call, and this gets blocked until QApplication::exit() or QApplication::quit() is called to terminate the loop. The wait_for_more_events() function blocks until some event is generated. This blocking is not a busy wait blocking and will not exhaust CPU resources. The event loops take cares of a lot of background activities, such as draw, redraw, click, press, notification; as well as your custom events, such as calling web services for data, and a lot more. Hence, it is very important not to block the event as failing as blocking will make the application freeze. Generally, the event loop can be awoken by a window manager activity, socket activity, timers, or events posted by other threads. All these activities require a running event loop.

It is more important not to block the event loop because when it is struck, widgets will not update themselves, timers won't fire, and networking communications will slow down and stop.

In short, your application will not respond to any external or internal events (because this code takes place behind the scenes of the event loop operation), and hence, it is advised to quickly react to events and return to the event loop as soon as possible.

Event processing

Qt offers five methods to perform event processing. They are as follows:

- Reimplementing a specific event handler, such as `keyPressEvent()`, and `paintEvent()`
- Reimplementing the `QObject::event()` class
- Installing an event filter on a single `QObject`
- Installing an event filter on the `QApplication` object
- Subclassing `QApplication` and reimplementing `notify()`

Generally, this can be broadly divided into reimplementing event handlers and installing event filters. We will look at each of them in detail.

Reimplementing event handlers

We can implement the task at hand or control a widget by reimplementing the virtual event handling functions. The following example will explain how to reimplement a few of the most commonly used events, such as a key press event, a mouse double-click event, and a window resize event. We will have a look at the code first and defer the explanation for after the code:

```
        # Import necessary modules
import sys
from PySide.QtGui import  QmainWindow, QApplication

# Our main widget class
class MyWidget(QWidget):
    # Constructor function
    def __init__(self):
        super.(MyWidget,self).__init__()
        self.initGUI()
```

```
        def initGUI(self):
            QWidget.__init__(self)
            self.setWindowTitle("Reimplementing Events")
            self.setGeometry(300, 250, 300, 100)
            self.myLayout = QVBoxLayout()
            self.myLabel = QLabel("Press 'Esc' to close this App")
            self.infoLabel = QLabel()
            self.myLabel.setAlignment(Qt.AlignCenter)
            self.infoLabel.setAlignment(Qt.AlignCenter)
            self.myLayout.addWidget(self.myLabel)
            self.myLayout.addWidget(self.infoLabel)
            self.setLayout(self.myLayout)
            self.show()

        # Function reimplementing Key Press, Mouse Click and Resize Events
        def keyPressEvent(self, event):
            if event.key() == Qt.Key_Escape:
                self.close()

        def mouseDoubleClickEvent(self, event):
            self.close()

        def resizeEvent(self, event):
            self.infoLabel.setText("Window Resized to QSize(%d, %d)" %
    (event.size().width(), event.size().height()))

    if __name__ =='__main__':
        # Exception Handling
        try:
            myApp = QApplication(sys.argv)
            myWidget = MyWidget()
            myApp.exec_()
            sys.exit(0)
        except NameError:
            print("Name Error:", sys.exc_info()[1])
        except SystemExit:
            print("Closing Window...")
        except Exception:
            print(sys.exc_info()[1])
```

In the preceding code, the keyPressEvent() function reimplements the event that is generated as a result of pressing a key. We implemented it in such a way that the application closes when the *Esc* key is pressed. On running this code, we will get an output that is similar to the one shown in the following screenshot:

The application will be closed if you press the *Esc* key. The same functionality is implemented on a mouse double-click event. The third event is a resize event. This event gets triggered when you try to resize the widget. The second line of text in the window will show the size of the window in (width, height) format. You could witness the same on resizing the window.

Similar to keyPressEvent(), we could also implement keyReleaseEvent() which would be triggered on release of the key. Normally, we are not very interested in the key release events except for the keys that are important. The specific keys for which the release event holds importance are the modifier keys, such as *Ctrl*, *Shift*, and *Alt*. These keys are called **modifier keys**, and they can be accessed using QKeyEvent::modifiers. For example, the key press of a *Ctrl* key can be checked using Qt.ControlModifier. The other modifiers are Qt.ShiftModifier and Qt.AltModifier. For instance, if we want to check the press event of a combination of the *Ctrl + PageDown* keys, we could perform the check as follows:

```
if event.key() == Qt.Key_PageDown and
event.modifiers() == Qt.ControlModifier:
    print("Ctrl+PgDn Key is pressed")
```

Before any particular key press or mouse click event handler function, say for example, keyPressEvent(), is called, the widget's event() function is called first. The event() method may handle the event itself, or it may delegate the work to a specific event handler, such as resizeEvent() or keyPressEvent(). The implementation of the event() function is very helpful in some special cases, such as the *Tab* key press event. In most cases, the widget with the keyboard that focuses the event() method will call setFocus() on the next widget in the tab order, and it will not pass the event to any of the specific handlers. So, we may have to reimplement any specific functionality for the *Tab* key press event in the event() function.

This behavior of propagating the key press events is the outcome of Qt's Parent-Child hierarchy. The event gets propagated to its parent, or its grandparent, and so on if it is not handled at any particular level. If the top-level widget also doesn't handle the event, it is safely ignored. The following code shows an example of how to reimplement the `event()` function:

```python
# Import necessary modules
import sys
from PySide.QtGui import *
from PySide.QtCore import *

# Our main widget class
class MyWidget(QWidget):
    # Constructor function
    def __init__(self):
        super(MyWidget, self).__init__()
        self.initGUI()

    def initGUI(self):
        self.setWindowTitle("Reimplementing Events")
        self.setGeometry(300, 250, 300, 100)
        self.myLayout = QVBoxLayout()
        self.myLabel1 = QLabel("Text 1")
        self.myLineEdit1 = QLineEdit()
        self.myLabel2 = QLabel("Text 2")
        self.myLineEdit2 = QLineEdit()
        self.myLabel3 = QLabel("Text 3")
        self.myLineEdit3 = QLineEdit()
        self.myLayout.addWidget(self.myLabel1)
        self.myLayout.addWidget(self.myLineEdit1)
        self.myLayout.addWidget(self.myLabel2)
        self.myLayout.addWidget(self.myLineEdit2)
        self.myLayout.addWidget(self.myLabel3)
        self.myLayout.addWidget(self.myLineEdit3)
        self.setLayout(self.myLayout)
        self.show()

    # Function reimplementing event() function
    def event(self, event):
        if event.type() == QEvent.KeyRelease and event.key() == Qt.Key_Tab:
            self.myLineEdit3.setFocus()
            return True
        return Qwidget.event(self, event)
```

In the preceding example, we try to mask the default behavior of the *Tab* key. If you haven't implemented the event() function, pressing the *Tab* key will have set the focus to the next available input widget. You will not be able to detect the *Tab* key press in the keyPress() function, as described in the previous examples, because the key press is never passed to them. Instead, we have to implement this in the event() function. If you execute the preceding code, you will see that every time you press the *Tab* key, the focus will be set into the third QLineEdit widget of the application. Inside the event() function, it is more important to return the value from the function. If we have processed the required operation, True is returned to indicate that the event is handled successfully; otherwise, we pass the event handling to the parent class's event() function.

As you noticed in Linux, the example allowed you to move the focus to the first text box and then shifted focus back to the third text box; and the event implementation is only for the KeyRelease event and not the KeyPress event. This is because keys, such as tab, arrow, and space, have special functionality and KeyPress is handled by the parent window handler and not passed onto the custom event handler that is defined. To handle these special events and others, we can use the event filter that is discussed next.

Installing event filters

An interesting and notable feature of Qt's event model is to allow a QObject instance to monitor the events of another QObject instance before the latter object is even notified of it. This feature is very useful in constructing custom widgets comprised of various widgets altogether. Consider that you have a requirement to implement a feature in an internal application for a customer such that pressing the *Enter* key must have to shift the focus to next input widget. One way to approach this problem is to reimplement the keyPressEvent() function for all the widgets present in the custom widget. Instead, this can be achieved by reimplementing the eventFilter() function for the custom widget. If we implement this, the events will first be passed on to the custom widget's eventFilter() function before being passed on to the target widget. An example is implemented as follows:

```
def eventFilter(self, receiver, event):
    if(event.type() == QEvent.MouseButtonPress):
        QMessageBox.information(None,"Filtered Mouse Press Event!!",
            'Mouse Press Detected')
        return True
    return super(MyWidget,self).eventFilter(receiver, event)
```

Remember to return the result of event handling, or pass it on to the parent's `eventFilter()` function. To invoke `eventFilter()`, it has to be registered as follows in the constructor function:

```
self.installEventFilter(self)
```

In the reimplementation of the event handler session, we discussed that key press events for keys, such as tab, arrow, and space, cannot be captured. The following code snippet will help you understand how `eventFilter` can be used to capture these key press events:

```
def eventFilter(self, receiver, event):
        if event.type()== QEvent.KeyPress and event.key()== Qt.Key_
Tab:
            self.myLineEdit3.setFocus()
            return True
        return super(MyWidget,self).eventFilter(receiver, event)
if __name__ =='__main__':
    # Exception Handling
    try:
        myApp = QApplication(sys.argv)
        myWidget = MyWidget()
        myApp.installEventFilter(myWidget)
        myApp.exec_()
        sys.exit(0)
    except NameError:
        print("Name Error:", sys.exc_info()[1])
    except SystemExit:
        print("Closing Window...")
    except Exception:
        print(sys.exc_info()[1])
```

There is also a change in the main function, the `installEventFilter` is moved from `MyWidget` to the main function, and the event is registered for `QApplication` level. Now, you can run the program and see how the difference in *Tab* press is handled.

Reimplementing the notify() function

The final way of handling events is to reimplement the `notify()` function of the
`QApplication` class. This is the only way to get all the events before any of the event
filters that were discussed previously are notified. The event gets notified to this
function first before it gets passed on to the event filters and specific event functions.
The use of `notify()` and other event filters is generally discouraged unless it is
absolutely necessary to implement them because handling them at top level might
introduce unwanted results, and we might end up handling the events that we don't
want to. Instead, use the specific event functions to handle events. The following
code excerpt shows an example of reimplementing the `notify()` function:

```
class MyApplication(QApplication):
  def __init__(self, args):
      super(MyApplication, self).__init__(args)

  def notify(self, receiver, event):
    if (event.type() == QEvent.KeyPress):
      QMessageBox.information(None, "Received Key Release EVent", "You
Pressed: "+ event.text())
    return super(MyApplication, self).notify(receiver, event)
```

Signals and slots

The fundamental part of any GUI program is the communication between the
objects. Signals and slots provide a mechanism to define this communication
between the actions that happened and the result that is proposed for the respective
action. Prior to Qt's modern implementation of signal or slot mechanism, older
toolkits achieved this kind of communication through callbacks. A callback is a
pointer to a function; so, if you want a processing function to notify about some
event, you pass a pointer to another function (the callback) to the processing
function. The processing function then calls the callback whenever appropriate. This
mechanism does not prove useful in the later advancements due to some flaws in the
callback implementation.

A signal is an observable event, or at least a notification that the event has happened. A slot is a potential observer; usually, it is a function that is called. In order to establish communication between them, we connect a signal to a slot to establish the desired action. We already saw the concept of connecting a signal to a slot in the earlier chapters while designing the text editor application. Those implementations handle and connect different signals to different objects. However, we may have different combinations, defined as follows:

- One signal can be connected to many slots
- Many signals can be connected to the same slot
- A signal can be connected to other signals
- Connections can be removed

PySide offers various predefined signals and slots such that we can connect a predefined signal to a predefined slot and do nothing else to achieve what we want. However, it is also possible to define our own signals and slots. Whenever a signal is emitted, Qt will simply throw it away. We can define the slot to catch and notice the signal that is being emitted. The first code excerpt that follows this text will be an example to connect predefined signals to predefined slots, and the latter will discuss the custom user-defined signals and slots.

The first example is a simple EMI calculator application that takes the Loan Amount, Rate of Interest, and Number of Years as its input, and calculates the EMI per month and displays it to the user. To start with, we set the components that are required for the EMI calculator application in a layout. The Amount will be a text input from the user. The Rate of Years will be taken from a spin box input or a dial input. A spin box is a GUI component, which has its minimum and maximum value set, and the value can be modified using the up and down arrow buttons present at its side. The dial represents a clock-like widget whose values can be changed by dragging the arrow. The Number of Years value is taken by a spin box input or a slider input:

```python
class MyWidget(QWidget):
    def __init__(self):
        QWidget.__init__(self)
        self.amtLabel = QLabel('Loan Amount')
        self.roiLabel = QLabel('Rate of Interest')
        self.yrsLabel = QLabel('No. of Years')
        self.emiLabel = QLabel('EMI per month')
        self.emiValue = QLCDNumber()
```

```
self.emiValue.setSegmentStyle(QLCDNumber.Flat)
self.emiValue.setFixedSize(QSize(130,30))
self.emiValue.setDigitCount(8)

self.amtText = QLineEdit('10000')
self.roiSpin = QSpinBox()
self.roiSpin.setMinimum(1)
self.roiSpin.setMaximum(15)
self.yrsSpin = QSpinBox()
self.yrsSpin.setMinimum(1)
self.yrsSpin.setMaximum(20)

self.roiDial = QDial()
self.roiDial.setNotchesVisible(True)
self.roiDial.setMaximum(15)
self.roiDial.setMinimum(1)
self.roiDial.setValue(1)
self.yrsSlide = QSlider(Qt.Horizontal)
self.yrsSlide.setMaximum(20)
self.yrsSlide.setMinimum(1)

self.calculateButton = QPushButton('Calculate EMI')


self.myGridLayout = QGridLayout()

self.myGridLayout.addWidget(self.amtLabel, 0, 0)
self.myGridLayout.addWidget(self.roiLabel, 1, 0)
self.myGridLayout.addWidget(self.yrsLabel, 2, 0)
self.myGridLayout.addWidget(self.amtText, 0, 1)
self.myGridLayout.addWidget(self.roiSpin, 1, 1)
self.myGridLayout.addWidget(self.yrsSpin, 2, 1)
self.myGridLayout.addWidget(self.roiDial, 1, 2)
self.myGridLayout.addWidget(self.yrsSlide, 2, 2)
self.myGridLayout.addWidget(self.calculateButton, 3, 1)

self.setLayout(self.myGridLayout)
self.setWindowTitle("A simple EMI calculator")
```

Until now, we set the components that were required for the application. Please note that the application layout uses a grid-layout option. The next set of code is also defined in the contructor's __init__ function of the `MyWidget` class, which will connect the different signals to slots. There are different ways that you can use a connect function. The code explains the various options that are available:

```
self.roiDial.valueChanged.connect(self.roiSpin.setValue)
self.connect(self.roiSpin, SIGNAL("valueChanged(int)"), self.
roiDial.setValue)
```

In the first line of the previous code, we connect the `valueChanged()` signal of `roiDial` to call the slot of `roiSpin`, `setValue()`. So, if we change the value of `roiDial`, it emits a signal that connects to the roiSpin's `setValue()` function, and it will set the value accordingly. Here, we must note that changing either the spin or dial must change the other value because both represent a single entity. Hence, we induce a second line that calls roiDial's `setValue()` slot on changing the roiSpin's value. However, it is to be noted that the second form of connecting signals to slots is deprecated. This is given here just for reference, and it is strongly discouraged to use this form. The following two lines of code execute the same for the Number of Years slider and spin:

```
self.yrsSlide.valueChanged.connect(self.yrsSpin.setValue)
self.connect(self.yrsSpin, SIGNAL("valueChanged(int)"), self.
yrsSlide, SLOT("setValue(int)"))
```

In order to calculate the EMI value, we connect the clicked signal of the push button to a function (slot) that calculates the EMI and displays it to the user:

```
self.connect(self.calculateButton, SIGNAL("clicked()"), self.
showEMI)
```

The EMI calculation and display function is given for your reference, as follows:

```
def showEMI(self):
    loanAmount = float(self.amtText.text())
    rateInterest = float( float (self.roiSpin.value() / 12) / 100)
    noMonths = int(self.yrsSpin.value() * 12)
    emi = (loanAmount * rateInterest) * ( ( ( (1 + rateInterest) **
noMonths ) / ( ( (1 + rateInterest) ** noMonths ) - 1) ))
    self.emiValue.display(emi)
    self.myGridLayout.addWidget(self.emiLabel, 4, 0)
    self.myGridLayout.addWidget(self.emiValue, 4, 2)
```

The sample output of the application is shown in the following screenshot:

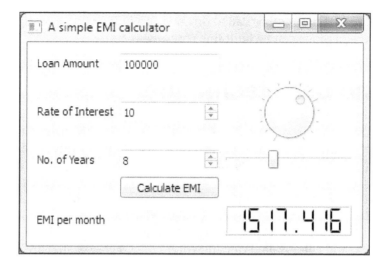

The EMI calculator application uses the predefined signals, such as `valueChanged()`, `clicked()`, and predefined slots, such as `setValue()`. However, the application also uses a user-defined `showEMI()` slot to calculate the EMI. As with slots, it is also possible to create a user-defined signal and emit it when required. The following program is an example to create and emit user-defined signals:

```
import sys
from PySide.QtCore import *

# define a new slot that receives and prints a string
def printText(text):
  print(text)

class CustomSignal(QObject):
  # create a new signal
  mySignal = Signal(str)


if __name__ == '__main__':
  try:
    myObject = CustomSignal()
    # connect signal and slot
    myObject.mySignal.connect(printText)
    # emit signal
    myObject.mySignal.emit("Hello, Universe!")
  except Exception:
    print(sys.exc_info()[1])
```

This is a very simple example of using custom signals. In the `CustomSignal` class, we create a signal named `mySignal`, and we emit it in the main function. We also define that the `printText()` slot will be called on emission of the `mySignal` signal. Many complex signal emissions can be built this way.

Drag and drop technique

There are various ways in which you can transfer data between two objects or applications. Drag and drop is a modern visual technique of transference of data between objects. It enables the user to copy and paste very intuitively. The drag and drop is a combination of two events, namely *Dragging* and *Dropping*. The widgets can serve as drag sites, drop sites, or as both. One of the important factors that we should take care of is the **MIME** type of the object that we would drag or drop. This is to ensure that the information can be transferred safely between applications. The various MIME types that are supported by Qt include plain text, HTML text, URI-list text, image data, and color data. We will explore the Qt classes that are used for this action and shortly test them with an example.

The various classes that are involved in drag and drop and their necessary MIME encoding and decoding are listed in the following table:

Class	Description
QDragEnterEvent	This provides an event that is sent to a widget when a drag and drop action enters it
QDragLeaveEvent	This provides an event that is sent to a widget when a drag and drop action leaves it
QDragMoveEvent	This provides an event that is sent to a widget when a drag and drop action is in progress
QDropEvent	This provides an event that is sent to a widget when a drag and drop action is completed
QMimeData	This provides a container for data that records information about its MIME type

A drag can be initiated by setting the widget's `setDragEnabled()` with a Boolean True value. The dropping functionality can be implemented by reimplementing the `dragMoveEvent()` and `dropEvent()` functions. As the user drags over the widget, `dragMoveEvent()` occurs, and `dropEvent()` occurs when the drag event is completed. We will now see an example for the drag and drop events and the working of the code will be explained in the following code:

```
cclass MyWidget(QWidget):
    def __init__(self):
        super(MyWidget,self).__init__()
        self.initGUI()

    def initGUI(self):
        self.myListWidget1 = MyListWidget(self,None)
        self.myListWidget2 = MyListWidget(self,'ICON')

        self.setGeometry(300, 350, 500, 150)

        self.myLayout = QHBoxLayout()
        self.myLayout.addWidget(self.myListWidget1)
        self.myLayout.addWidget(self.myListWidget2)

        self.myListWidget1.additem('blue_bird.png',"Angry Bird Blue")
        self.myListWidget1.additem('red_bird.png',"Angry Bird Red")
        self.myListWidget1.additem('green_bird.png',"Angry Bird
Green")
        self.myListWidget1.additem('black_bird.png',"Angry Bird
Black")
        self.myListWidget1.additem('white_bird.png',"Angry Bird
White")

        self.myListWidget2.additem('gray_pig.png', "Grey Pig")
        self.myListWidget2.additem('brown_pig.png', "Brown Pig")
        self.myListWidget2.additem('green_pig.png', "Green Pig")

        self.setWindowTitle('Drag and Drop Example');

        self.setLayout(self.myLayout)
        self.show()

class MyListWidget(QListWidget):

    def __init__(self,parent=None,viewMode=None):
        super(MyListWidget,self).__init__(parent)
        self.initWidget(viewMode)

    def initWidget(self,viewMode=None):
        self.setAcceptDrops(True)
        self.setDragEnabled(True)
        if viewMode == 'ICON':
            self.setViewMode(QListWidget.IconMode)

    def additem(self,fileName, desc):
        QListWidgetItem(QIcon(fileName), desc, self)
```

The preceding program will look like the following screenshot on execution:

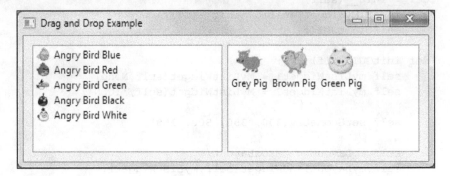

Both partitions of the application have a QListWidget object with some items added to it. The left side is the default view mode of QListWidget, and the right side is set to icon view mode. Both these widgets support the dragging mode as they are set with setDragEnabled(True). They also accept the dropping functionality as the setAcceptDrops(True) is set. You can test this by dragging-and-dropping between the widgets. We can control the behavior of the application by reimplementing the previously discussed event handler functions.

Drawing shapes

The PySide.QtGui.QPainter class performs low-level painting on widgets and other paint devices. The QPainter class provides all the functions to draw simple lines to more complex shapes. This class also provides settings to render quality images and supports clipping. The drawing is usually done within the widget's paintEvent() function. The drawing functionalities are placed in between the begin() and end() functions of the QPainter object. The QPainter object is initialized with the constructor, customized with some set functions, such as pen style and brush style, and then the draw function is called. The QPainter. isActive() function indicates whether the painter is active. The QPainter object is activated when QPainter.begin() is invoked and deactivated on calling QPainter. end().

The various drawings are performed using the QPainter's draw functions. The `QPainter` has three important settings that set the appearance of the drawing. They are as follows:

- **Pen**: This is used to draw lines, shapes, and outlines. It takes various settings to draw that include color, width, line style, and so on
- **Brush**: This is used to pattern fill geometric shapes. The various settings that a brush can take include color, style, texture, gradient, and so on
- **Font**: This is mainly used to draw Unicode text. The font settings include font style, font family, and point size

The settings for these parameters can be set and modified anytime by calling the `setFont()`, `setBrush()`, and `setFont()` on QPainter with their respective QPen, QBrush, or QFont objects.

In this section, we are going to explore the most commonly used drawing shapes. The following table will give you a gist of the available draw functions of the QPainter object:

Constant	Description
drawPoint()	This draws a single point at the given position
drawText()	This draws the given text within the defined rectangle
drawLine()	This draws a line between two pairs of points
drawRect()	This draws a rectangle
drawRoundedRect()	This draws a rectangle with rounded edges or corners
drawEllipse()	This draws an ellipse that is defined by the given rectangle
drawArc()	This draws an arc that is defined by the given rectangle
drawPie()	This draws a pie that is defined by the given rectangle
drawChord()	This draws a chord that is defined by the given rectangle
drawPolyline()	This draws a polyline that is defined by the given points
drawPolygon()	This draws a polygon that is defined by the given points
drawConvexPolygon()	This draws a convex polygon that is defined by the given polygon
drawImage()	This draws the given image inside the given rectangle
drawPath()	This draws the given painter path that is defined by the QPainterPath
drawPicture()	This draws the given picture

All the earlier-listed functions take various arguments as their parameters for different drawing functionalities. Also, all these drawing functions use the current pen, brush, and text settings to draw the objects. This section is not enough to cover and discuss all the different types of drawing functions, and hence, we should look at a sample program that is self-explanatory and exhibits the different styles of the listed functions. The complete version of the basic drawing functionality code can be downloaded from this book's site. Here, we just display the contents of the `paintEvent()` function with different drawing shapes. The complete code is bundled with event handling that we have discussed in the first section of this chapter and the usage of other built-in widgets, such as combobox, that we will discuss in the next chapter. As of now, it is sufficient if you can understand the reimplementation of the event handlers and drawing functions of the program:

```
def paintEvent(self, event):
    rect = QRect(10, 20, 80, 60)

    startAngle = 30 * 16
    arcLength = 120 * 16

    painter = QPainter()
    painter.begin(self)
    painter.setPen(self.pen)
    painter.setBrush(self.brush)
    if self.shape == PaintArea.Line:
        painter.drawLine(rect.bottomLeft(), rect.topRight())
    elif self.shape == PaintArea.Points:
        painter.drawPoints(PaintArea.points)
    elif self.shape == PaintArea.Polyline:
        painter.drawPolyline(PaintArea.points)
    elif self.shape == PaintArea.Polygon:
        painter.drawPolygon(PaintArea.points)
    elif self.shape == PaintArea.Rect:
        painter.drawRect(rect)
    elif self.shape == PaintArea.RoundRect:
        painter.drawRoundRect(rect)
    elif self.shape == PaintArea.Ellipse:
        painter.drawEllipse(rect)
    elif self.shape == PaintArea.Arc:
        painter.drawArc(rect, startAngle, arcLength)
    elif self.shape == PaintArea.Chord:
        painter.drawChord(rect, startAngle, arcLength)
    elif self.shape == PaintArea.Pie:
```

```
        painter.drawPie(rect, startAngle, arcLength)
      elif self.shape == PaintArea.Path:
        painter.drawPath(path)
      elif self.shape == PaintArea.Text:
        painter.drawText(rect, QtCore.Qt.AlignCenter, "Basic Drawing
  Widget")
      painter.end()
```

This will produce a window, as displayed in the following screenshot. You can select the choice of your drawing from the comboboxes, and it will be painted in the application.

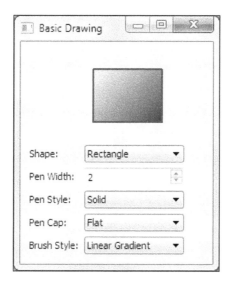

Graphics and effects

We could create any custom graphics that we like by creating a custom widget and by reimplementing its paint event. This approach is very helpful when we are trying to create some small graphics, such as drawing graphs or to draw basic shapes. In order to create animations and more complex graphics, we will take help from the PySide's graphics view classes, which are explained as follows:

- **QGraphicsScene**: This provides a surface to manage a large number of 2D graphical items

- **QGraphicsItem**: This serves as the base class for all graphical items, such as ellipses, lines, and so on, in a graphics scene

- **QGraphicsView**: This provides a widget to display the contents of a graphics scene

The graphic view classes can be used by creating a scene that is represented by a QGraphicsScene object first. Scenes can be associated with the QGraphicsView object to represent or view on the screen. Items that are represented by the QGraphicsItem object can be added to the scene. A scene is created, items are added, and visualized, in that order. QGraphicsView can be triggered to visualize a whole scene or only a part of it by changing the bounding rectangle values. These interactions can happen using the mouse or a keyboard. The graphics view translates the mouse and key events into scene events represented by QGraphicsSceneEvent and forwards them to the visualized scene. The custom scene interactions are achieved by reimplementing the mouse and key event handlers. The most interesting feature of the graphics views is that we can apply transformations to them, such as scaling and rotation. This can be done without changing the original scene's items:

```python
class MyView(QGraphicsView):
    def __init__(self):
        QGraphicsView.__init__(self)

        self.myScene = QGraphicsScene(self)
        self.myItem = QGraphicsEllipseItem(-20, -10, 50, 20)
        self.myScene.addItem(self.myItem)
        self.setScene(self.myScene)

        self.timeLine = QTimeLine(1000)
        self.timeLine.setFrameRange(0, 100)
        self.animate = QGraphicsItemAnimation()
        self.animate.setItem(self.myItem)
        self.animate.setTimeLine(self.timeLine)

        self.animate.setPosAt(0, QPointF(0, -10))
        self.animate.setRotationAt(1, 360)

        self.setWindowTitle("A Simple Animation")
        self.timeLine.start()
```

This program will create an animated ellipse as its output. As discussed, we created a scene, added items to it, and displayed it via the view class. The animation is supported by the QGraphicsAnimationItem() object. Many more complex animations can be built on top of this but explaining them is beyond the scope of this book. You can explore them by yourself in order to create more QGrapicsView objects and complex animations.

The `PySide.QtGui.QGraphicsEffect` class serves as the base class for the graphical effects on an application. With the help of effects, we can alter the appearance of elements. The graphical effects objects operate between the sources, for example, a pix map item and the destination—the viewport, and render the respective effects for the image. The various graphical effects that Qt provides are as follows:

- **QGrpahicsBlurEffect**: This blurs the item by a given radius
- **QGraphicsDropShadowEffect**: This renders a drop shadow behind the item
- **QGraphicsColorizeEffect**: This renders the item in shades of any given color
- **QGraphicsOpacityEffect**: This renders the item with a specified opacity

All these classes are inherited from the `QGraphicsEffect` base class. The following code excerpt shows an example of adding effects to the items:

```
self.effect = QGraphicsDropShadowEffect(self)
self.effect.setBlurRadius(8)
self.myItem.setGraphicsEffect(self.effect)
self.myItem.setZValue(1)
```

When this effect is added, you will notice a shadow in the animated ellipse, as shown in the following screenshot. Similarly, other effects can be added to the items.

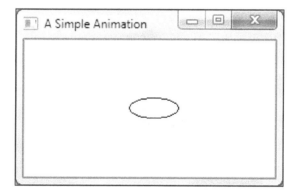

Summary

This chapter was a real rollercoaster ride as we went into the depths of PySide programming. We started with discussing event handlers and reimplementation techniques to achieve the task at hand. We also discussed event filters and reimplementing the `notify()` function. Unless absolutely necessary, the latter forms of reimplementing events should be avoided to make an efficient program.

We then explored a very fundamental mechanism of Qt, signals and slots. The signals and slots mechanism follows an observer pattern listening and binding to objects when called. We started with implementing the built-in signals and slots. Later in this section, we implemented and emitted our own custom signals and also discussed how to listen to them.

In the latter half, we shifted our focus to diagrams and graphics. Starting with the drag and drop functionality usage, we also saw various types of QPainter draw objects. The chapter ended with a brief discussion on graphics and effects. The examples that are shown in the latter half of the chapter are very basic examples to help you understand the basic concepts. Much more complex applications can be designed, and this would by itself be the subject matter for a complete book. In the next chapter, we will learn about using dialogs and widgets to build a complete and usable GUI application.

5
Dialogs and Widgets

Most, if not all, GUI applications that are developed have to be supplemented with dialogs and widgets to enable different use cases and workflows for the user. Dialogs are usually small-sized windows with specific functionalities that aid the users with selecting or executing some operation. The most common examples of dialogs include the **File Open** dialog in many text and image editing applications, the **Color Chooser** dialog in various paint applications, and so on. In many GUI toolkits, the terms dialogs and widgets are used interchangeably. As a general difference, dialogs are the small windows whose main purpose is to establish a connection between the user and the program. We normally use dialog boxes to receive an input from the users or to represent an output or error message to the users. However, widgets are collections of the building blocks of the applications, such as buttons, check boxes, progress bars, and so on. This chapter will introduce you to some of the built-in dialogs and widgets that Qt provides us. Moving on, we will develop a customized **Find** dialog that will add to the text-editor program that we developed in *Chapter 3*, *Main Windows and Layout Management*. We will also develop a customized **Analog Clock** widget.

In this chapter, we will be covering the following topics:

- Built-in dialogs
- Custom dialogs
- Widgets at a glance
- Custom widgets
- Implementation of MDI

Built-in dialogs

Qt provides a rich set of built-in dialogs. They are as follows:

- `QFileDilaog`: This provides the user with a dialog that allows them to select files or directories

- `QErrorMessage`: This provides the user with a dialog that displays error messages

- `QColorDialog`: This provides the user with a dialog to specify or choose between colors

- `QPrintDialog`: This provides the user with a dialog that aids in printer and printing configuration

- `QPageSetupDialog`: This provides the user with a dialog that manages configuration for the page-related options on a printer

- `QWizard`: This provides a dialog framework for wizards

- `QProgressDialog`: This provides feedback on the progress of a slow operation

- `QPrintPreviewDialog`: This provides a dialog to preview and configure page layouts for printer output

- `QMessageBox`: This provides a dialog that is usually used to display modal information to the user requiring approval or cancellation

- `QInputDialog`: This provides a simple convenience dialog to get a single value from the user

- `QFontDialog`: This provides a dialog widget to select a font

In this section, we will discuss the implementations of some widely used widgets. A few of the widgets, such as `QMessageBox`, `QFontDialog`, and `QErrorMessage`, have already been introduced to you in some of the preceding chapters.

QFileDialog

The `PySide.QtGui.QFileDialog` class provides a dialog that allows users to select files or directories. It helps users to traverse the native file system in order to select one or many files or directories. The easy and best way to create a file dialog is to use the static functions that are provided by the `QFileDialog` class. A sample use of static function is given as follows:

```
fileName = QFileDialog.getOpenFileName(self,
"Open Files", "c:/", "Text
files(*.txt)")
```

In this example, the file dialog was created using a static getOpenFileName function. Initially, this function call will create a file dialog with the path mentioned in the third parameter of the function. The fourth parameter restricts the type of file that has to be shown in the dialog to open it. The first parameter takes the value of the parent to the dialog, and the second is used to display a title for the dialog. The filters that are represented in the fourth parameter can take multiple values depending on the type of file that is to be filtered. Please note that the values must be separated by a ;; delimiter. An example for the filter can look like the following line:

```
"Images (*.png *.jpg);; Text files (*.txt);; Word documents(*.doc)"
```

The following code shows an example to create the file dialog in a menu option. The program is self-explanatory and is based on the concepts that we saw in the third chapter of this book:

```
import sys
from PySide.QtGui import *
from PySide.QtCore import *

class MyFileDialog(QMainWindow):

    def __init__(self):
        QMainWindow.__init__(self)

        self.textEdit = QTextEdit()
        self.setCentralWidget(self.textEdit)
        self.statusBar()

        openFile = QAction(QIcon('open.png'), 'Open', self)
        openFile.setShortcut('Ctrl+O')
        openFile.setStatusTip('Open new File')
        openFile.triggered.connect(self.showDialog)

        menubar = self.menuBar()
        fileMenu = menubar.addMenu('&File')
        fileMenu.addAction(openFile)

        self.setGeometry(300, 300, 350, 300)
        self.setWindowTitle('Example - File Dialog')
        self.show()

    def showDialog(self):
        fileName, _ = QFileDialog.getOpenFileName(self, "Open Text
Files", "c:/", "Text files(*.txt)")
```

```
            contents = open(fileName, 'r')

            with contents:
                data = contents.read()
                self.textEdit.setText(data)


if __name__ =='__main__':
    # Exception Handling
    try:
        myApp = QApplication(sys.argv)
        myFD = MyFileDialog()
        myFD.show()
        myApp.exec_()
        sys.exit(0)
    except NameError:
        print("Name Error:", sys.exc_info()[1])
    except SystemExit:
        print("Closing Window...")
    except Exception:
        print(sys.exc_info()[1])
```

 If you run this program, you will witness that a file open dialog is opened on triggering the `File->Open` option in the menu bar.

The file dialog can also be created without using the static functions by directly creating an instance of the `QFileDialog` class that is explained, as follows:

```
fileDialog = QFileDialog(self)
fileDialog.setFileMode(QFileDialog.AnyFile)
fileDialog.setNameFilter("Text files(*.txt)")
```

The second line of the preceding code sets the mode of the file dialog to Any File, which means that the user can specify a file that doesn't even exist in the filesystem. This mode is very useful when we want to create a Save As dialog. The other modes that the file dialog can take are as follows:

- `QFileDialog.ExistingFile`: This is used if the user must select an existing file

- `QFileDialog.Directory`: This is used if the user must select only a directory and not files

- `QFileDialog.ExistingFile`: This is used if the user wants to select more than one file

The third line depicts how to set the filters for the file dialog as explained in the previous program. Also, the file dialog has two view modes, namely, **View** and **Detail**. As the name indicates, the list view just displays the name of the files and directories in a list, but the detail mode enhances it with additional details about the file, such as file size, date modified, and so on.

QInputDialog

The `PySide.QtGui.QInputDialog` class provides a very easy and convenient dialog to receive input from the users. The input can be a text string, a number, or an item from the list. A label is provided with the input box to indicate to the user what they have to enter. To enable this, four convenient functions are used, as follows:

- `QInputDialog.getText()`: This receives a text or string from the user
- `QInputDialog.getInteger()`: This receives an integer value as an input
- `QInputDialog.getDouble()`: This receives a float value as an input with double-precision accuracy
- `QInputDialog.getItem()`: This receives a particular selectable value from the list of items

The dialog is provided with two buttons, **OK** and **Cancel**, to accept or reject values respectively:

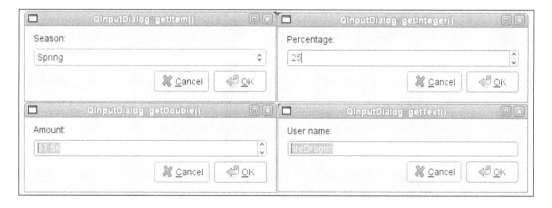

The following code explains the use of various input dialogs:

```
# Import necessary modules
import sys
from PySide.QtGui import *
from PySide.QtCore import *
```

```python
class MyInputDialog(QWidget):

    def __init__(self):

        QWidget.__init__(self)
        self.myNameButton = QPushButton('Name', self)
        self.myNameButton.clicked.connect(self.showNameDialog)

        self.myAgeButton = QPushButton('Age', self)
        self.myAgeButton.clicked.connect(self.showAgeDialog)

        self.myChoiceButton = QPushButton('Choice', self)
        self.myChoiceButton.clicked.connect(self.showChoiceDialog)

        self.myNameLE = QLineEdit(self)
        self.myAgeLE = QLineEdit(self)
        self.myChoiceLE = QLineEdit(self)

        self.myLayout = QFormLayout()
        self.myLayout.addRow(self.myNameButton, self.myNameLE)
        self.myLayout.addRow(self.myAgeButton, self.myAgeLE)
        self.myLayout.addRow(self.myChoiceButton, self.myChoiceLE)

        self.setLayout(self.myLayout)
        self.setGeometry(300, 300, 290, 150)
        self.setWindowTitle('Input Dialog Example')
        self.show()

    def showNameDialog(self):
        text, ok = QInputDialog.getText(self, 'Input Text Dialog',
            'Enter your name:')

        if ok:
            self.myNameLE.setText(str(text))

    def showAgeDialog(self):
        text, ok = QInputDialog.getInteger(self, 'Input Number
Dialog',
            'Enter your age:')

        if ok:
            self.myAgeLE.setText(str(text))
```

```
def showChoiceDialog(self):
    strList = ['Ice Cream', 'Choclates', 'Milk Shakes']
    text, ok = QInputDialog.getItem(self, 'Input Combo Dialog',
        'Enter your choice:', strList)

    if ok:
        self.myChoiceLE.setText(str(text))

if __name__ =='__main__':
    # Exception Handling
    try:
        myApp = QApplication(sys.argv)
        myID = MyInputDialog()
        myID.show()
        myApp.exec_()
        sys.exit(0)
    except NameError:
        print("Name Error:", sys.exc_info()[1])
    except SystemExit:
        print("Closing Window...")
    except Exception:
        print(sys.exc_info()[1])
```

In the preceding code, each button's click event is connected to a slot that presents it to the user with different types of input dialogs. The values of the dialogs reflect on the **Line Edit** box upon clicking the **OK** button.

QColorDialog

The `PySide.QtGui.QColorDialog` provides a dialog to choose and specify colors. The color dialog is mainly used in the paint applications to allow the user to set the color of the brush or paint an area with a specific color. This dialog can also be used to set text colors in text-based applications. As with the other dialogs, we use a static `QColorDialog.getColor()` function to show the dialog and subsequently allow the user to select a color from the dialog. This dialog can also be used to allow the users to select the color transparency by passing some additional parameters. It is also possible to set and remember the custom colors and share them between color dialogs in an application. The code that follows is a short example of using the color dialog:

```
class MyColorDialog(QWidget):

    def __init__(self):
```

```
            QWidget.__init__(self)
            myColor = QColor(0, 0, 0)

            self.myButton = QPushButton('Press to Change Color', self)
            self.myButton.move(10, 50)

            self.myButton.clicked.connect(self.showColorDialog)

            self.myFrame = QFrame(self)
            self.myFrame.setStyleSheet("QWidget { background-color: %s }"
                % myColor.name())
            self.myFrame.setGeometry(130, 22, 100, 100)

            self.setGeometry(300, 300, 250, 180)
            self.setWindowTitle('Color Dialog - Example')
            self.show()

    def showColorDialog(self):

        color = QColorDialog.getColor()

        if color.isValid():
            self.myFrame.setStyleSheet("QWidget { background-color: %s
}"
                % color.name())
```

The preceding example will show a button that when pressed shows a color dialog.
The color can be selected, and the same is painted in the frame that is used for this
purpose.

QPrintDialog

The PySide.QtGui.QPrintDialog provides a dialog to specify the user's printer
configuration. The configuration includes document-related settings, such as the
paper size and orientation, type of print, color or grayscale, range of pages, and
number of copies to print. The configuration settings also allow the user to select the
type of printer from the printers that are available, including any configured network
printers. The QPrintDialog objects are constructed with a PySide.QtGui.QPrinter
object and executed using the exec_() function. The printer dialog uses the native
system of display and configuration. The following example shows a crude way of
creating a print dialog. The refined implementation is left as an exercise for you to
explore. A sample implementation can be downloaded from the code snippets that
come along with this book:

```
def printDoc(self):
        document = QTextDocument("Sample Page")
        printer = QPrinter()

        myPrintDialog = QPrintDialog(printer, self)
        if myPrintDialog.exec_() != QDialog.Accepted:
            return
    document.print_(printer)
```

Custom dialogs

We saw some examples of the built-in dialogs in the previous section. The need may arise in a real application scenario to define and create a custom dialog that is based on the user's requirement. **Qt** provides the support to create custom-based dialogs and use it, in addition to the various built-in dialogs. In this section, we are going to explore how to create a custom **Find** dialog for our text editor application that we created in *Chapter 3*, *Main Windows and Layout Management*. The Find Dialog class is inherited from the QDialog class and defines the properties to implement search functionality. Once the find dialog functions are defined, it can be added to our text editor application, and the slots are implemented accordingly.

In order to create a **Find** dialog, we must create an outline of what it will look like. The following is a sample look of how we would want our Find dialog to appear:

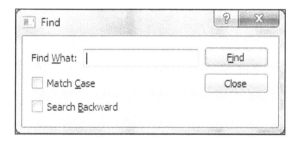

This is a very simple **Find** dialog. We would want to capture the text that has to be searched using a line edit dialog. The two checkboxes, **Match Case** and **Search Backward**, try to catch the user's choices. The button press events are connected to specific slots to perform the desired action. We used the layout concepts that were introduced to you in the previous chapter to place the widgets:

```
class FindDialog(QDialog):

    def __init__(self):
        QDialog.__init__(self)
        self.findLabel = QLabel("Find &What:")
```

```python
        self.lineEdit = QLineEdit()
        self.findLabel.setBuddy(self.lineEdit)

        self.caseCheckBox = QCheckBox("Match &Case")
        self.backwardCheckBox = QCheckBox("Search &Backward")

        self.findButton = QPushButton("&Find")
        self.findButton.setDefault(True)
        self.closeButton = QPushButton("Close")

        self.topLeftLayout = QHBoxLayout()
        self.topLeftLayout.addWidget(self.findLabel)
        self.topLeftLayout.addWidget(self.lineEdit)

        self.leftLayout = QVBoxLayout()
        self.leftLayout.addLayout(self.topLeftLayout)
        self.leftLayout.addWidget(self.caseCheckBox)
        self.leftLayout.addWidget(self.backwardCheckBox)

        self.rightLayout = QVBoxLayout()
        self.rightLayout.addWidget(self.findButton)
        self.rightLayout.addWidget(self.closeButton)
        self.rightLayout.addStretch()

        self.mainLayout = QHBoxLayout()
        self.mainLayout.addLayout(self.leftLayout)
        self.mainLayout.addLayout(self.rightLayout)

        self.findButton.clicked.connect(self.findText)
        self.setWindowTitle("Find")
        self.setLayout(self.mainLayout)
        self.show()

    def findText(self):
        mySearchText = self.lineEdit.text()
        if self.caseCheckBox.isChecked():
            caseSensitivity = Qt.CaseSensitive
        else:
            caseSensitivity = Qt.CaseInsensitive
        if self.backwardCheckBox.isChecked():
            #search functionality goes here...
            print("Backward Find ")
        else:
            #search functionality goes here...
            print("Forward Find")
```

In order to use this dialog, simply create an instance of `MyFindDialog` that will create a **Find** dialog, as shown in the following lines of code.

```
def findDialog(self):
        myFindDialog = FindDialog()
        myFindDialog.exec_()
```

Thus, we can create and customize the dialog according to the needs of our application.

Widgets at a glance

Widgets are the basic building blocks of a *Graphical User Interface* hierarchy in GUI applications. Widgets are basically used to display data and status information, receive user input, and provide a container for other widgets that should be grouped together. Qt comes with a variety of basic and advanced built-in widgets that can be customized to our own needs. A list of predefined widgets is given in the following tables for your reference. `QWidget` is the base class for all the widgets given in the following lists.

The following is a list of predefined basic widgets:

Widget	Description
QCheckBox	This is a checkbox with a text label
QComboBox	This is a combined button and pop-up list
QCommandLinkButton	This is a Vista-style command-link button
QDateEdit	This is a widget that is used to edit dates that are based on the QDateTimeEdit widget
QDateTimeEdit	This is a widget that is used to edit dates and times
QDial	This is a rounded range control (such as a speedometer or potentiometer)
QDoubleSpinBox	This is a spin box widget that takes doubles
QFocusFrame	This is a focus frame, which can be outside of a widget's normal paintable area
QFontComboBox	This is a combobox that lets the user select a font family
QLCDNumber	This displays a number with LCD-like digits
QLabel	This is text or image display
QLineEdit	This is a one-line text editor
QMenu	This is the menu widget for use in menu bars, context menus, and other popup menus
QProgressBar	This is a horizontal or vertical progress bar

Widget	Description
QPushButton	This is a command button
QRadioButton	This is a radio button with a text label
QScrollArea	This allows scrolling view onto another widget
QScrollBar	This is a vertical or horizontal scroll bar
QSizeGrip	This is a resize handle to resize top-level windows
QSlider	This is a vertical or horizontal slider
QSpinBox	This is a spin box widget
QTabBar	This is a tab bar, for example, for use in tabbed dialogs
QTabWidget	This is a stack of tabbed widgets
QTimeEdit	This is a widget that is used to edit times that are based on the QDateTimeEdit widget
QToolBox	This is a column of tabbed widget items
QToolButton	This is a quick-access button to commands or options that are usually used inside a QToolBar
QWidget	This is the base class of all user interface objects

The following is a list of predefined advanced widgets:

Widget	Description
QCalendarWidget	This is a monthly-based calendar widget allowing the user to select a date
QColumnView	This is a model/view implementation of a column view
QDataWidgetMapper	This is a mapping between a section of a data model to widgets
QDesktopWidget	This allows access to screen information on multihead systems
QListView	This allows list or icon view onto a model
QMacCocoaViewContainer	This is a widget for Mac OS X that can be used to wrap arbitrary Cocoa views (that is, NSView subclasses) and insert them into Qt hierarchies
QMacNativeWidget	This is a widget for Mac OS X that provides a way to put Qt widgets into Carbon or Cocoa hierarchies depending on how Qt was configured
QTableView	This is the default model/view implementation of a table view
QTreeView	This is the default model/view implementation of a tree view

Widget	Description
QUndoView	This displays the contents of a QUndoStack
QWSEmbedWidget	This enables embedded top-level widgets in Qt for Embedded Linux
QWebView	This is a widget that is used to view and edit web documents
QX11EmbedContainer	This is the XEmbed container widget
QX11EmbedWidget	This is the XEmbed client widget
Phonon::VideoWidget	This is a widget that is used to display video

The following is a list of predefined organizer widgets:

Widget	Description
QButtonGroup	This is a container that is used to organize groups of button widgets
QGroupBox	This is a group box frame with a title
QSplitter	This implements a splitter widget
QSplitterHandle	This will handle functionality of the splitter
QStackedWidget	This is a stack of widgets where only one widget is visible at a time
QTabWidget	This is a stack of tabbed widgets

We saw the implementation of a few of these built-in widgets in our previous chapters. One of the greatest strengths of PySide lies in the ease of creation of customized widgets. We can group some of the basic widgets together to create a customized widget on our own. Before we can do this, we also have several ways to customize a widget to suit our needs. The basic form of customization is to change the properties of the existing widget. We can also opt to use style sheets to customize the widget's appearance and some aspects of its behavior. In some cases, it is highly likely that we may require a widget that is different from any of the standard widgets. In these cases, we can subclass QWidget directly and can completely define the behavior and appearance of the widget ourselves. In the next example, we create a customized Analog Clock widget and demonstrate how to create custom widgets.

Custom widget

To start with, we define the AnalogClock class that is inherited from QWidget. We define two variables that will be used to draw the hourHand and minuteHand of the analog clock. We also define the colors for the pointers:

```
class AnalogClock(QWidget):
    hourHand = QPolygon([
        QPoint(7, 8),
        QPoint(-7, 8),
        QPoint(0, -40)
    ])

    minuteHand = QPolygon([
        QPoint(7, 8),
        QPoint(-7, 8),
        QPoint(0, -70)
    ])

    hourColor = QColor(255, 0, 127)
    minuteColor = QColor(0, 127, 127, 255)
```

Next, we define an init function that will start the timer that will update the clock on the expiry of every minute. It also resizes the widget and sets a title for it:

```
def __init__(self, parent=None):
    QWidget.__init__(self)

    timer = QTimer(self)
    timer.timeout.connect(self.update)
    timer.start(1000)

    self.setWindowTitle("Analog Clock")
    self.resize(200, 200)
```

The core functionality of the analog clock is defined in the paintEvent() function, which would be called on the update function of the analog clock widget. We call the QTime.CurrentTime() function to update the current time from the system. The next set of lines will set the pen properties and draws the minute hand and hour hand polygons along with the line indications of the analog clock:

```
def paintEvent(self, event):
    side = min(self.width(), self.height())
    time = QTime.currentTime()

    painter = QPainter(self)
    painter.setRenderHint(QPainter.Antialiasing)
```

```
painter.translate(self.width() / 2, self.height() / 2)
painter.scale(side / 200.0, side / 200.0)

painter.setPen(Qt.NoPen)
painter.setBrush(AnalogClock.hourColor)

painter.save()
painter.rotate(30.0 * ((time.hour() + time.minute() / 60.0)))
painter.drawConvexPolygon(AnalogClock.hourHand)
painter.restore()

painter.setPen(AnalogClock.hourColor)

for i in range(12):
    painter.drawLine(88, 0, 96, 0)
    painter.rotate(30.0)

painter.setPen(Qt.NoPen)
painter.setBrush(AnalogClock.minuteColor)

painter.save()
painter.rotate(6.0 * (time.minute() + time.second() / 60.0))
painter.drawConvexPolygon(AnalogClock.minuteHand)
painter.restore()

painter.setPen(AnalogClock.minuteColor)

for j in range(60):
    if (j % 5) != 0:
        painter.drawLine(92, 0, 96, 0)
    painter.rotate(6.0)
```

On running the preceding application, we will see an analog clock widget drawn, as given in the following screenshot:

Implementation of MDI

We have already discussed the differences between SDI and MDI applications in *Chapter 3, Main Windows and Layout Management*. We saw many implementations of SDI applications. In this section, we will explore a technique of creating MDI applications.

A Multiple Document Interface application will consist of a main window where multiple child windows and dialogs reside and appear for interaction. The central widget can be either the PySide.QtGui.QMdiArea or PySide.QtGui.QWorkSpace widget. They are by themselves widget components that manage the central area of the main window to arrange the MDI windows in a layout. Subwindows are then created and added to the MDI area or a workspace. An example of the MDI application is given as follows:

```
class MyMDIApp(QMainWindow):

    def __init__(self):
        QMainWindow.__init__(self)

        workspace = QWorkspace()
        workspace.setWindowTitle("Simple WorkSpace Example")

        for i in range(5):
            textEdit = QTextEdit()
            textEdit.setPlainText("Dummy Text " * 100)
            textEdit.setWindowTitle("Document %i" % i)
            workspace.addWindow(textEdit)

        workspace.tile()
        self.setCentralWidget(workspace)

        self.setGeometry(300, 300, 600, 350)
        self.show()
```

The MDI windows inside a main windowed application can be set in a cascade or tile layout by default or a customized layout can be specified. The following screenshots show the two types of layout of the example application:

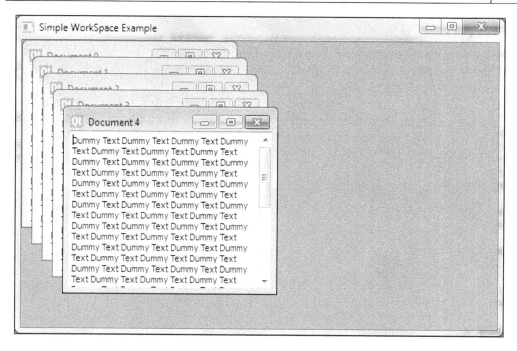

The following screenshot depicts another layout for the display of the child windows:

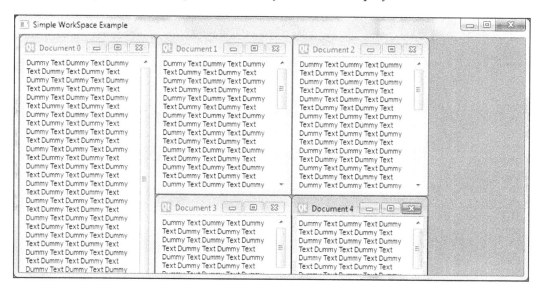

Summary

The beauty of any programming language lies in its capability to customize things for better use other than its rich library of predefined objects. PySide exhibits its dynamics by allowing the users to explore a variety of predefined dialogs and widgets and also facilitating extremely easy ways to create and use customized ones. This chapter has taken you through the various dialogs and widgets and also taught you how to build them on your own. In the next chapter, we will see how to connect our application to databases and access information out of them.

6

Database Handling

Most of the applications that we use in our day-to-day life have to deal with some type of stored data that can be used as and when required. Databases enable us to store this data in a structured manner and also provide us with some guidelines on how this data is to be presented to the end users. In short, databases are an organized body of related information that is usually intro records with a common denominator. The software that controls the access to the databases and enables you to create, edit, and maintain them is known as **Database Management Systems (DBMS)**. There are numerous DBMS systems that are available in the market and each of them is used to suit some specific needs.

The DBMS that we use in this chapter to provide examples is SQLite. As the name specifies, SQLite is a light-weight, public-domain, in-process database system that is used for local storage in many application software applications. This chapter assumes that the users are familiar with **SQL (Structured Query Language)**, which is used to access the data, and have some knowledge in model/view programming. The **QtSql** module of PySide provides a database-independent interface to access SQL databases. So, apart from the initial connection and some other raw SQL syntax, almost all other queries work with any SQL database.

Connecting to the database

A database connection is represented by the PySide.QtSql.QSqlDatabase class. This class provides an interface to access a database through the connection. The connection is accomplished through Qt's supported database drivers, which are derived from the PySide.QtSql.QSqlDriver class. The QSqlDriver class is an abstract base class to access specific SQL Databases and should be used with QSqlDatabase. As with any other PySide feature that supports customization, it is also possible to create our own SQL drivers by subclassing the QSqlDriver class and reimplementing its virtual functions.

Before explaining the concept of connecting to databases, we will look at the types of database access that is provided by PySide. The access is provided at two levels, a high-level access using QSqlTableModel or QSqlRelationalTableModel, and a low-level access using QSqlQuery. The former one uses model/view architecture and provides a high-level interface from which to read and write database records from a table. The latter one is based on executing and manipulating SQL queries directly on the QSqlDatabase class. This class can accept the **Data Manipulation Language (DML)** statements, such as SELECT, INSERT, UPDATE, and DELETE, as well as **Data Definition Language (DDL)** statements, such as CREATE, ALTER, and DROP. It can also be used to execute database-specific commands that are not standard SQL, for example, SET DATESTYLE=ISO for PostgreSQL.

The connection to the database in an application can take place at any point when it is required to. But, in most of the applications it is done after the creation of the QApplication object and before the main form is created or shown. This way, we can inform users about the unsuccessful connection prior and, thus, prevent them from executing database-specific actions that will otherwise crash or cause an exception in our program. A connection is created by calling the static QSqlDatabase.addDatabase() function by giving the name of the database driver that we want to use and, optionally, a connection name. A database connection is identified by the connection name that we specify and not by the database name.

 It is possible for us to create multiple database connections at a time and differentiate them from each other by the connection name.

It is also correct to create a connection without a name by making it a default connection. Once a connection object has been created, we can move on to set other necessary attributes, such as the database's name, username, password, host, and port details, and other connect options, if necessary. Once this is completed, we can activate the connection to the database with the help of the QSqlDatabase.open() function call. The following code presents the series of steps that we discussed in creating and activating a connection:

```
db = QSqlDatabase.addDatabase("QMYSQL")
db.setHostName("testServer")
db.setDatabaseName("sampledb")
db.setUserName("test")
db.setPassword("pass123")
ok = db.open()
```

In the preceding code, the addDatabase() function can be given an optional second parameter, which specifies the connection name that is given, as follows:

```
db = QSqlDatabase.addDatabase("QMYSQL", "myConn")
```

However, when using SQLite, it is enough to specify only the database name (SQLite is a local storage database implementation and normally does not require a password). Usually, this will normally be a filename, but it can be the special name, **:memory:**, to specify to use an in-memory database. When the open() call is executed on the connection, the file will be created if it does not exist in prior. So, the code to connect to the SQLite database using the SQLite driver for PySide, QSQLITE, is as follows:

```
db = QSqlDatabase.addDatabase("QSQLITE")
db.setDatabaseName("test.db")
ok = db.open()
```

This will create a connection to the SQLite **test.db** database file. We should take care of handling the connection errors by checking the return value of the db.open() function.

 It is a good practice to notify the users upfront about any errors.

Once the connection is established, we can get the list of the tables, its primary index, and meta-information about the table's fields with their specific functions. The QSqlDatabase.removeDatabase() function is called with a connection name to remove a connection.

Executing SQL queries

After successful connection to the database, we can execute SQL queries to perform some actions on it. If we don't specify a connection name, the default connection is taken. The PySide.QtSql.QSqlQuery class provides a means of executing and manipulating SQL databases.

Executing a query

The SQL query can be executed by creating a `QSqlQuery` object and calling an `exec_()` function on this. As an example, we create a table named `employee` and define its columns, as follows:

```
myQuery = QSqlQuery()

myQuery.exec_("""CREATE TABLE employee (id INTEGER PRIMARY KEY
AUTOINCREMENT UNIQUE NOT NULL, first_name CHAR(20) NOT NULL, last_name
CHAR(20), age INT, sex CHAR(1), income FLOAT)""")
```

This will create a table with six columns, namely id, first_name, last_name, age, sex, and income. The `QSqlQuery` constructor accepts an optional parameter, a `QSqlDatabase` object that specifies which database connection to use. As we don't specify any connection name in the preceding code, the default connection is used. In case of any errors, the `exec_()` function returns false, and the error details are available in `QSqlQuery.lastError()`.

Inserting, updating and deleting records

In this section, we will look at the different ways in which we can execute DML commands. A simple form of inserting the values in the table that we created in our previous section is given as follows:

```
myQuery = QSqlQuery()
myQuery.exec_("""INSERT INTO employee (first_name, last_name, age,
sex, income) VALUES ('Alice', 'M', 30, 'F', 5000.00)""")
```

This will insert a single row in the employee table. This method is easier if you need to insert a single row into the table. However, if we require the creation of many rows, it is advised to separate the query from the actual values being used. This can be achieved with the use of placeholders by binding the values with the columns in the table. Qt supports two types of placeholder systems, namely, named binding and positional binding. This way of constructing queries is also called *prepared queries*.

An example of the named binding is given as follows:

```
myQuery.prepare("INSERT INTO employee (first_name, last_name, age,
sex, income) VALUES (:first_name, :last_name, :age, :sex, :income)")

for fname, lname, age, sex, income in data:
myQuery.bindValue(":first_name", fname)
myQuery.bindValue(":last_name", lname)
```

```
myQuery.bindValue(":age", age)
myQuery.bindValue(":sex", sex)
myQuery.bindValue(":income", income)

myQuery.exec_()
```

> Please note that the id column is omitted during the insertion of rows in the previous examples because we have defined it to the AUTOINCREMENT values while creating the table. This means that whenever we insert a new value and database, implementation will automatically take care of creating a new ID entry that is a +1 increment of the previous one that was inserted.

Now, let's look at the other type of prepared query, positional binding:

```
myQuery.prepare("INSERT INTO employee (first_name, last_name, age,
sex, income) VALUES (?, ?, ?, ?, ?)")

for fname, lname, age, sex, income in data:
myQuery.addBindValue(fname)
myQuery.addBindValue (lname)
myQuery.addBindValue (age)
myQuery.addBindValue (sex)
myQuery.addBindValue (income)

myQuery.exec_()
```

Both methods work with all database drivers that are provided by Qt. Prepared queries improve performance on databases that support them. Otherwise, Qt simulates the placeholder syntax by preprocessing the query. The actual query that gets executed can be received by calling the `QSqlQuery.executedQuery()` function.

> Please note that you need to call `QSqlQuery.prepare()` only once, and you can call `bindValue()` or `addBindValue()` followed by `exec_()` as many times as necessary. Another advantage of the prepared queries besides performance is that we can specify arbitrary values without worrying about escaping the special characters. Escaping special character is required to prevent an SQL query that is composed out of a possible user-provided value to inject code that will break the program, or breach the security of stored records.

QSqlQuery can execute any arbitrary SQL statements, such as SELECT and INSERT statements. So, updating and deleting records is as easy as executing the corresponding queries. For example, we can update a record, as shown in the following line:

```
myQuery.exec_("UPDATE employee SET income=7500.00 WHERE id=5")
```

Similarly, we can delete a record, as follows:

```
myQuery.exec_("DELETE FROM employee WHERE id=8")
```

Successfully executed SQL statements set the query's state to active and can be retrieved from QSqlQuery.isActive(). Otherwise, it is set to inactive. This method will return a Boolean value, True or False, depending on the success of the operation.

Navigating records

The next feature that we are about to discuss is how to navigate the records of the result set of a SELECT query. Navigating the records is performed by the following functions:

- PySide.QtSql.QSqlQuery.next()

- PySide.QtSql.QSqlQuery.previous()

- PySide.QtSql.QSqlQuery.first()

- PySide.QtSql.QSqlQuery.last()

- PySide.QtSql.QSqlQuery.seek()

These functions help us in iterating back and forth through the records. However, if we need to move only forward through the results, we can set the QSqlQuery. setForwardOnly(), which can improve performance and save a significant amount of memory in some databases. The QSqlQuery.value() function takes an integer positional argument, which returns the value of the field index in the current record. The fields are numbered from left to right using the text of the SELECT statement. For example, in the following query, field 0 represents the first_name, and field 1 represents the last_name.

```
SELECT first_name. last_name FROM employee
```

As QSqlQuery.value() takes an index positional argument, it is not advised to use SELECT * in the query. Instead, use the column names because we will not know the order of columns in the SELECT * query.

Let's now take a look at an example of navigating the records through the result set:

```
myQuery.exec_("SELECT id, first_name, income FROM employee")
while myQuery.next():
id = myQuery.value(0).toInt()
name = myQuery.vaue(1).toString()
salary = myQuery.value(2).toInt()
```

In the preceding example, we use the `toInt()` and `toString()` functions to convert the result to a specific data type because all the values that are returned are of the `QVariant` type, which can hold various data types, such as `int`, `string`, `datetime`, and so on.

Before closing the section on executing SQL queries, we will look at a few more useful functions that the `QSqlQuery` class offers.

The `QSqlQuery.numRowsAffected()` function will return the number of rows that are affected by the result of an `UPDATE` or `DELETE` query. This function return -1 if it cannot be determined or the query is not active. In case of the `SELECT` statements, this function returns undefined. Instead, we use `QSqlQuery.size()` which will return the size of the result set. This function also returns -1 if the size cannot be determined, or if the database does not support reporting information about query sizes, or if the query is not active.

`QSqlQuery.finish()` will instruct the database driver that no more data will be fetched from the query until it is re-executed. Usually, we do not call this function until we want to free some resources, such as locks or cursors, if you intend to reuse the query at a later time. Finally, we can call `QSqlQuery.at()` to retrieve the current row index.

Database transactions

In order to check whether the database driver uses a specific feature, we can use `QSqlDriver.hasFeature()`, which will return a true or false value accordingly. So, we can use `QSqlDriver.hasFeatire(QSqlDriver.Transactions)` to identify whether the underlying database engine supports transactions. If the underlying database supports transactions, we can retrieve the commit and rollback results using the `QSqlDatabase.commit()` and `QSqlDatabase.rollback()` respectively. The transaction can be initiated using the `QSqlDatabase.transaction()` call. Transactions can be used to ensure that a complex operation is atomic or to provide a means of cancelling a complex change in the middle.

Table and form views

This section is devoted to explaining the representation of data in a form view or a table view. But, before that, we can look at some examples of accessing databases through high-level model classes. The following classes are available in Qt for this purpose.

- QSqlQueryModel: This provides a read-only data model for SQL result sets
- QSqlTableModel: This provides an editable data model for a single database table
- QSqlRelationalTableModel: This provides an editable data model for a single database table with foreign key support

Let's view some quick examples of each of these classes.

QSqlQueryModel

This model aims at providing a high-level interface to execute SQL queries and traverse the result set. This class is built on top of the QSqlQuery class and can be used to provide data to view classes, such as QTableView, which we are going to discuss in the forthcoming sections. A sample program using QSqlQueryModel is given as follows:

```
model = QSqlQueryModel()
model.setQuery("SELECT fname FROM employee")
print("Names of Employee")
while i < model.rowcount() :
   print(model.record(i).value( "fname").toString())
```

In the example shown, we set the the query using the model.setQuery() function. Once the query is set, the QSqlQueryModel.record(int) method is used to get individual records.

QSqlTableModel

The PySide.QtSql.QSqlTableModel class provides an editable data model for a single database table. As with QSqlQueryModel, this class also provides a high-level interface and can be used to provide data to view class. The only difference is that it allows the editing of data, which QSqlQueryModel does not support. A sample program is given as follows for your reference:

```
model =  QSqlTableModel()
model.setTable("employee")
```

```
model.setFilter("age > 40")
model.setEditStrategy(QSqlTableModel.OnManualSubmit)
model.select()
model.removeColumn(0) # to remove the id column
while i < model.rowcount() :
  print(model.record(i))
```

This works in the same way as explained in our previous example. The main difference to note here is Line 4. The `QSqlTableModel.setEditStarategy()` function describes which strategy we prefer to use to edit values in the database. The various options that this function can take are given as follows:

Constant	Description
`::QSqlTableModel.OnFieldChange`	This means that the changes to a model will be applied immediately to the database
`QSqlTableModel.OnRowChange`	This means that the changes on a row will be applied when the user selects a different row
`QSqlTableModel.OnManualSubmit`	All changes will be cached in the model until either `PySide.QtSql.QSqlTableModel.submitAll()` or `PySide.QtSql.QSqlTableModel.revertAll()` is called

Please note that to prevent inserting partial values on a row into the database, **onFieldChange** will behave like **onRowChange** for newly inserted rows. The `QSqlTableModel.setFilter()` function executes the functionality of a WHERE clause in SQL queries. If the model is already selected and populated, the `setFilter()` will refilter the results. The `QSqlTableModel.setRecord()` function is used to modify a row, `QSqlTabelModel.removeRows(int)` is used to delete rows from the table.

QSqlRelationalTableModel

The `PySide.QtSql.QSqlRelationalTableModel` class serves the same purpose as `QSqlTableModel` with additional foreign key support. An example of this model is deferred to the last section after discussing the table and form views.

Table view

In the preceding sections, we discussed various model classes. Now, we will look at how to present the data to the users using the QTableView widget. The data source for the QTableView is provided by any of the model classes. The table view is the most used view format as this represents a virtual representation of 2D SQL table structure. We will look at the code first, then discuss its functionality:

```
import sys
from PySide.QtGui import *
from PySide.QtCore import *
from PySide.QtSql import *

def initializeModel(model):
    model.setTable("employee")

    model.setEditStrategy(QSqlTableModel.OnManualSubmit)
    model.select()

    model.setHeaderData(0, Qt.Horizontal, "ID")
    model.setHeaderData(1, Qt.Horizontal, "First Name")
    model.setHeaderData(2, Qt.Horizontal, "Last Name")
    model.setHeaderData(3, Qt.Horizontal, "Age")
    model.setHeaderData(4, Qt.Horizontal, "Gender")
    model.setHeaderData(5, Qt.Horizontal, "Income")

def createView(title, model):
    view = QTableView()
    view.setModel(model)
    view.setWindowTitle(title)
    return view

def createConnection():
    db = QSqlDatabase.addDatabase('QSQLITE')
    db.setDatabaseName('sample.db')

    ok = db.open()

    if not ok:
        return False

    myQuery = QSqlQuery()
```

```
    myQuery.exec_("""CREATE TABLE employee (id INTEGER PRIMARY KEY
                AUTOINCREMENT UNIQUE NOT NULL, first_name CHAR(20)
NOT NULL,
                last_name CHAR(20), age INT, sex CHAR(1), income
FLOAT)""")
    myQuery.exec_("""INSERT INTO employee (first_name, last_name, age,
sex, income)
                VALUES ('Alice', 'A', 30, 'F', 5000.00)""")
    myQuery.exec_("""INSERT INTO employee (first_name, last_name, age,
sex, income)
                VALUES ('Bob', 'B', 31, 'M', 5100.00)""")
    myQuery.exec_("""INSERT INTO employee (first_name, last_name, age,
sex, income)
                VALUES ('Caesar', 'C', 32, 'F', 5200.00)""")
    myQuery.exec_("""INSERT INTO employee (first_name, last_name, age,
sex, income)
                VALUES ('Danny', 'D', 34, 'M', 5300.00)""")
    myQuery.exec_("""INSERT INTO employee (first_name, last_name, age,
sex, income)
                VALUES ('Eziekel', 'E', 35, 'F', 5400.00)""")
    return True



if __name__ =='__main__':
    try:
        myApp = QApplication(sys.argv)

        if not createConnection():
            print("Error Connecting to Database")
            sys.exit(1)

        model = QSqlTableModel()
        initializeModel(model)

        view1 = createView("Table Model - Example1", model)
        view2 = createView("Table Model - Example2", model)

        view1.setGeometry(100, 100, 500, 220)
        view2.setGeometry(100, 100, 500, 220)
        view1.show()
        view2.move(view1.x() + view1.width() + 20, view1.y())
        view2.show()
        myApp.exec_()
        sys.exit(0)
    except NameError:
```

```
        print("Name Error:", sys.exc_info()[1])
    except SystemExit:
        print("Closing Window...")
    except Exception:
        print(sys.exc_info()[1])
```

At first, we create and establish a database connection and execute the sample data in the `createConnection()` function. As discussed, a SQLite connection is created using the Qt's SQLite driver, `QSQLITE`. We set the database name in the next line. If the file exists, the database connection uses it or else creates a new file using the same name. We check the success of the connection and return false if it is not so. The sample queries are executed one by one in order, and a true value is returned indicating that the connection was successful and the data is populated. In the `initializeModel()` function, we define the properties of the model and set the display format by specifying its column headers. The `createView()` function creates a view, and returns it to the caller function. On execution, we will get two table views, as shown in the following screenshot.

 Please note that on editing one view, the other gets updated. However, this does not update the table as we have set the edit strategy to **Manual Submit**.

On execution, we will get two table views, as shown in the following screenshot:

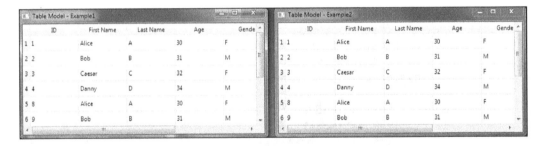

Form view

The form view is useful when you want to traverse the records one by one and perform some modifications to it. In this section, we will look at how to create a dialog form that displays, and we will also learn about how to add, edit, and delete records using the form dialog. We will use the same `employee` table that was created in our previous example.

We will not discuss the layout that is used in this program as our main aim is to discuss the form view. The model is created using the `QSqlTableModel`, setting the sort factor with the `first_name` column in the ascending order:

```
self.model = QSqlTableModel(self)
        self.model.setTable("employee")
        self.model.setSort(FIRST_NAME, Qt.AscendingOrder)
        self.model.select()
```

Next, we set the mapping of the form values with the column using the `QDataWidgetMapper` class. This class is used to provide mapping between a section of a data model to widgets. The `addMapping(widget, section)` function maps the widget to the section from the model. The section represents a column if the orientation is **Vertical**; otherwise, it represents a row. Finally, the `toFirst()` function populates the widget from the data from the first row of the model if the orientation is **Horizontal**; otherwise, it populates it from the first column:

```
self.mapper = QDataWidgetMapper(self)
self.mapper.setSubmitPolicy(QDataWidgetMapper.ManualSubmit)
self.mapper.setModel(self.model)
self.mapper.addMapping(firstNameEdit, FIRST_NAME)
self.mapper.addMapping(lastNameEdit, LAST_NAME)
self.mapper.addMapping(ageEdit, AGE)
self.mapper.addMapping(genderEdit, SEX)
self.mapper.addMapping(incomeEdit, INCOME)
self.mapper.toFirst()
```

Then, we connect the buttons to their respective slots:

```
self.connect(firstButton, SIGNAL("clicked()"),
                    lambda: self.saveRecord(EmployeeForm.FIRST))
self.connect(previousButton, SIGNAL("clicked()"),
                    lambda: self.saveRecord(EmployeeForm.PREV))
self.connect(nextButton, SIGNAL("clicked()"),
                    lambda: self.saveRecord(EmployeeForm.NEXT))
self.connect(lastButton, SIGNAL("clicked()"),
                    lambda: self.saveRecord(EmployeeForm.LAST))
self.connect(addButton, SIGNAL("clicked()"), self.addRecord)
self.connect(deleteButton, SIGNAL("clicked()"),
                    self.deleteRecord)
self.connect(quitButton, SIGNAL("clicked()"), self.done)
The slots are defined as follows:
    def done(self, result=None):
```

```python
        self.mapper.submit()
        QDialog.done(self, True)


    def addRecord(self):
        row = self.model.rowCount()
        self.mapper.submit()
        self.model.insertRow(row)
        self.mapper.setCurrentIndex(row)


    def deleteRecord(self):
        row = self.mapper.currentIndex()
        self.model.removeRow(row)
        self.model.submitAll()
        if row + 1 >= self.model.rowCount():
            row = self.model.rowCount() - 1
        self.mapper.setCurrentIndex(row)


    def saveRecord(self, where):
        row = self.mapper.currentIndex()
        self.mapper.submit()
        if where == EmployeeForm.FIRST:
            row = 0
        elif where == EmployeeForm.PREV:
            row = 0 if row <= 1 else row - 1
        elif where == EmployeeForm.NEXT:
            row += 1
            if row >= self.model.rowCount():
                row = self.model.rowCount() - 1
        elif where == EmployeeForm.LAST:
            row = self.model.rowCount() - 1
        self.mapper.setCurrentIndex(row)
```

The complete program can be downloaded from the code snippets that come along with this book. On execution, we will be presented with a dialog that is shown as follows, with which we can add, edit, or delete records:

Viewing relations in table views

The main feature of relational databases is their ability to relate one or more tables. One such relationship feature is the use of foreign key concept where a primary key of a table is related to a column in another table. This relation can be easily exhibited using `QRelationalTableModel`. In order to explain this, we create three tables that are connected to each other. The schema is defined as follows:

```
CREATE TABLE employee (id INTEGER PRIMARY KEY AUTOINCREMENT UNIQUE NOT
NULL, name VARCHAR(40) NOT NULL, department INTEGER, branch INTEGER)
CREATE TABLE department (id INTEGER PRIMARY KEY AUTOINCREMENT UNIQUE
NOT NULL, name VARCHAR(20) NOT NULL, FOREIGN KEY(id) REFERENCES
employee)
CREATE TABLE branch (id INTEGER PRIMARY KEY AUTOINCREMENT UNIQUE NOT
NULL, name VARCHAR(20) NOT NULL, FOREIGN KEY(id) REFERENCES employee)
```

If we use the `QSqlTableModel`, we will get a view as given in the following screenshot:

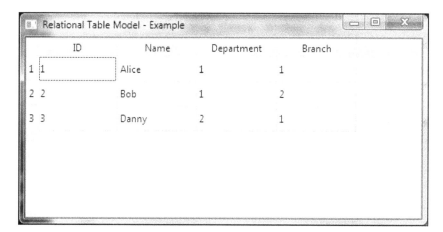

Using relational table model, we can reference the department and branch into their relations, which is given as follows:

```
model.setRelation(2, QSqlRelation("department", "id", "name"));
model.setRelation(3, QSqlRelation("branch", "id", "name"));
```

This code will set the relation of department and branch column to their respective tables along with what column value has to be displayed on the view. On setting the relation, the view will be modified, as shown in the following screenshot, where the IDs are resolved into their respective names.

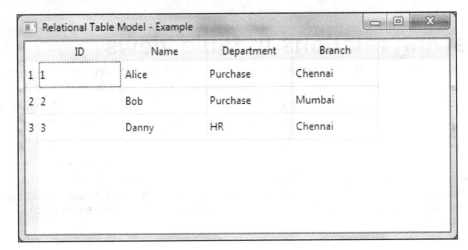

Thus, the relational model is so helpful in exhibiting relational databases.

Summary

Almost every application has to deal with databases for data storage and retrieval. Thus, it is valuable for a GUI developer to know about database interactions. Qt is supplemented with many built-in database drivers, which we can use to connect to the databases and perform desired operations. Also, with its wide variety of model and view classes, it becomes straight forward and hassle free for any GUI programmer to add persistent storage.

Index

A

about box
  creating 29, 30
absolute positioning 51
API Extractor
  about 7
  URL 7
application icon
  creating 19-24

B

built-in dialogs
  about 88
  QColorDialog 93
  QFileDialog 88-91
  QInputDialog 91, 93
  QPrintDialog 94
button
  adding 26-28

C

central widget 44

D

database connection 105, 106
Database Management Systems
    (DBMS) 105
database transactions
  about 111
  table and form views 112
Data Definition Language (DDL)
    statement 106

Data Manipulation Language (DML)
    statement 106
dialogs
  custom 95-97
drag and drop
  implementing 78-80
  QDragEnterEvent class 78
  QDragLeaveEvent class 78
  QDragMoveEvent class 78
  QDropEvent class 78
  QMimeData class 78

E

effects
  implementing 83-85
  QGraphicsColorizeEffect 85
  QGraphicsDropShadowEffect 85
  QGraphicsOpacityEffect 85
  QGrpahicsBlurEffect 85
event loop 66
event management
  about 65, 66
  event loop 66, 67
  event processing 67
event processing
  about 67
  event filters, installing 71, 72
  event handlers, reimplementing 67-71
  notify() function, reimplementing 73
exception handler 12
exception handling 12-14

F

form view 112, 116-118

G

Generator Runner
about 7
URL 7
Graphical User Interface (GUI)
about 2, 3
controls 3
graphics
creating 83-85
GUI applications 37

H

Hello World application
creating 9-11
Homebrew 5

L

layout containers 51, 52
layout management
about 50
absolute positioning 51
layout containers 51, 52
QBoxLayout class 52, 53
QFormLayout class 56
QGridLayout class 55
QStackedLayout class 56
Linux
PySide, building on 7
PySide, installation 5

M

Mac OS X
PySide, building on 8
PySide, installation 4
MacPorts 5
main window
creating 38, 39
MDI
implementation 102

menu bar

menu bar
about 43
adding 45
central widget 44
menus, adding 46-49
MIME type 78
modifier keys 69
Multiple Document Interface (MDI) 57

N

notify() function
reimplementing 73

O

Object-Oriented Design principles 15

P

PySide
about 2, 37
building 7, 8
building, on Linux 7
building, on Mac OS X 8
building, on Windows 6
Hello World application, creating 9-11
installation, on Linux 5
installation, on Mac OS X 4
installation, on Windows 4
objects, importing 8, 9
prerequisites, for Linux 7
prerequisites, for Windows 6
setting up 4
PySide Binaries MacOSX
URL 4
PySide Binaries Windows
URL 4
Pyside Mobility 2
PySide Qt Bindings
about 7
URL 7
Python
references 1

Q

QBoxLayout class
  about 52, 53
  QHBoxLayout class 53
  QVBoxLayout class 54
QColorDialog 88, 93
QErrorMessage 88
QFileDialog 88-91
QFormLayout class 56
QGraphicsItem class 83
QGraphicsScene class 83
QGraphicsView class 83
QGridLayout class 55
QIcon class, modes
  QIcon.Active 22
  QIcon.Disabled 22
  QIcon.Normal 22
  QIcon.Selected 22
QIcon class, state parameter
  QIcon.Off 23
  QIcon.On 23
QInputDialog 88, 91, 93
QMainWindow class 37
QMessageBox 88
QPageSetupDialog 88
QPainter object
  drawArc() function 81
  drawChord() function 81
  drawConvexPolygon() function 81
  drawEllipse() function 81
  drawImage() function 81
  drawLine() function 81
  drawPath() function 81
  drawPicture() function 81
  drawPie() function 81
  drawPoint() function 81
  drawPolygon() function 81
  drawPolyline() function 81
  drawRect() function 81
  drawRoundedRect() function 81
  drawText() function 81
QPainter object, settings
  Brush 81
  Font 81
  Pen 81

QPrintDialog 88, 94
QPrintPreviewDialog 88
QProgressDialog 88
QSqlQueryModel 112
QSqlRelationalTableModel 112, 113
QSqlTableModel 112, 113
QStackedLayout class 56
QtSql module 105
QWidget 15
QWizard 88

R

Rapid Application Development 1

S

setSegmentStyle() function, values
  QLCDNumber.Filled 33
  QLCDNumber.Flat 33
  QLCDNumber.Outline 33
shapes
  drawing 80-83
Shiboken Generator
  about 7
  URL 7
signals 73-78
simple text editor
  implementation 57, 62
Simple Text Editor application 46
Single Document Interface (SDI) 57
slots 73-78
SQL queries
  database transactions 111
  executing 107, 108
  records, deleting 108, 109
  records, inserting 108, 109
  records, navigating 110, 111
  records, updating 108, 109
SQL (Structured Query Language) 105
status bar
  about 39
  adding 39-42
status bar, information categories
  Normal 40
  Permanent 40
  Temporary 40

T

table views
about 112-116
relations, viewing 119, 120
time
tracking, timers used 30-33
toolbar 50
tooltip
displaying 24

W

What You See Is What You Get (WYSIWYG) 3
widgets
about 97
basic widgets 97, 98
custom widget 100, 101
predefined advanced widgets 98
predefined organizer widgets 99
WIMP 3
window
centering, on screen 28, 29
creating 15-18
Windows
PySide, building on 6
PySide, installation 4
Windows style
using 34
WYSIWYG viewer/editor 44

Z

Z-order 15

Thank you for buying
PySide GUI Application Development
Second Edition

About Packt Publishing

Packt, pronounced 'packed', published its first book, *Mastering phpMyAdmin for Effective MySQL Management*, in April 2004, and subsequently continued to specialize in publishing highly focused books on specific technologies and solutions.

Our books and publications share the experiences of your fellow IT professionals in adapting and customizing today's systems, applications, and frameworks. Our solution-based books give you the knowledge and power to customize the software and technologies you're using to get the job done. Packt books are more specific and less general than the IT books you have seen in the past. Our unique business model allows us to bring you more focused information, giving you more of what you need to know, and less of what you don't.

Packt is a modern yet unique publishing company that focuses on producing quality, cutting-edge books for communities of developers, administrators, and newbies alike. For more information, please visit our website at www.packtpub.com.

About Packt Open Source

In 2010, Packt launched two new brands, Packt Open Source and Packt Enterprise, in order to continue its focus on specialization. This book is part of the Packt Open Source brand, home to books published on software built around open source licenses, and offering information to anybody from advanced developers to budding web designers. The Open Source brand also runs Packt's Open Source Royalty Scheme, by which Packt gives a royalty to each open source project about whose software a book is sold.

Writing for Packt

We welcome all inquiries from people who are interested in authoring. Book proposals should be sent to author@packtpub.com. If your book idea is still at an early stage and you would like to discuss it first before writing a formal book proposal, then please contact us; one of our commissioning editors will get in touch with you.

We're not just looking for published authors; if you have strong technical skills but no writing experience, our experienced editors can help you develop a writing career, or simply get some additional reward for your expertise.

PySide GUI Application Development

ISBN: 978-1-84969-959-4   Paperback: 140 pages

Develop more dynamic and robust GUI applications using an open source cross-platform UI framework

1. Designed for beginners to help them get started with GUI application development.

2. Develop your own applications by creating customized widgets and dialogs.

3. Written in a simple and elegant structure to help you easily understand how to program various GUI components.

Python Multimedia

ISBN: 978-1-84951-016-5   Paperback: 292 pages

Learn how to develop Multimedia applications using Python with this practical step-by-step guide

1. Use Python Imaging Library for digital image processing.

2. Create exciting 2D cartoon characters using Pyglet multimedia framework.

3. Create GUI-based audio and video players using QT Phonon framework.

4. Get to grips with the primer on GStreamer multimedia framework and use this API for audio and video processing.

Please check **www.PacktPub.com** for information on our titles

Expert Python Programming

ISBN: 978-1-84719-494-7   Paperback: 372 pages

Best practices for designing, coding, and distributing your Python software

1. Learn Python development best practices from an expert, with detailed coverage of naming and coding conventions.

2. Apply object-oriented principles, design patterns, and advanced syntax tricks.

3. Manage your code with distributed version control.

4. Profile and optimize your code.

Python 3 Object Oriented Programming

ISBN: 978-1-84951-126-1   Paperback: 404 pages

Harness the power of Python 3 objects

1. Learn how to do Object Oriented Programming in Python using this step-by-step tutorial.

2. Design public interfaces using abstraction, encapsulation, and information hiding.

3. Turn your designs into working software by studying the Python syntax.

4. Raise, handle, define, and manipulate exceptions using special error objects.

Please check **www.PacktPub.com** for information on our titles

9 781785 282454